Epidemics

Look for these and other books in the Lucent Overview Series:

Abortion
Alcoholism
Artificial Organs
The Brain
Cancer
Cloning
Depression
Diabetes
Drug Abuse
Eating Disorders

Epidemics
Euthanasia
Genetic Engineering
Health Care
Memory
Mental Illness
Organ Transplants
Smoking
Suicide

Epidemics

by Lisa Yount

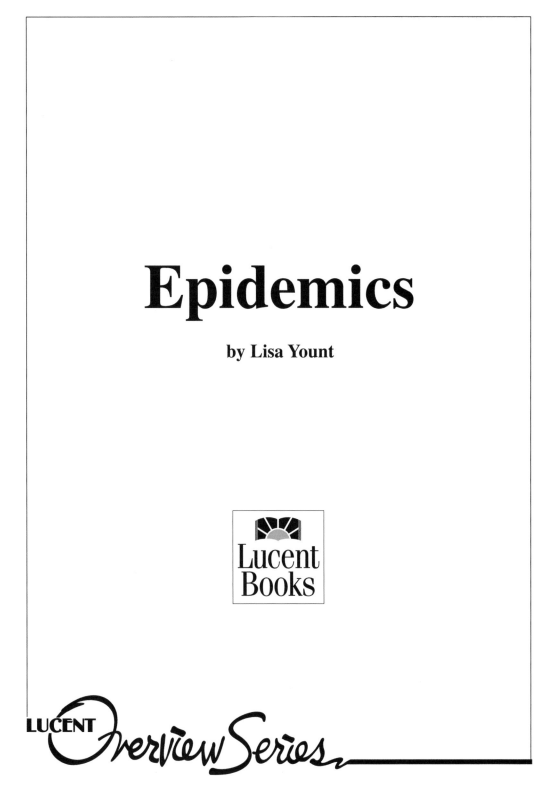

Lucent
Books

LUCENT *Overview Series*

LUCENT *Overview Series*

in memory of
Bruce Henderson

Library of Congress Cataloging-in-Publication Data

Yount, Lisa.
    Epidemics / by Lisa Yount.
        p.   cm. — (Lucent overview series)
    Includes bibliographical references and index.
    Summary: Discusses the return of epidemics in modern times,
possible causes, and how they are tracked and controlled.
    ISBN 1-56006-441-2 (lib. bdg.: alk. paper)
    1. Epidemiology Juvenile literature.   [1. Epidemiology.
2. Epidemics.]   I. Title.   II. Series.
RA653.5.Y68   2000
614.4'2—dc21   99-27458
                                                              CIP

Copyright © 2000 by Lucent Books, Inc.
P.O. Box 289011, San Diego, CA 92198-9011
Printed in the U.S.A.

Contents

Introduction

Father abandoned child, wife husband, one brother another. . . . They died by the hundreds, both day and night, and all were thrown in ditches and covered with earth. And as soon as those ditches were filled, more were dug. . . . I, Agnolo di Tura . . . buried my five children with my own hands.[1]

THESE WORDS, WRITTEN by a man from the Italian city of Siena, are one of many heartrending descriptions left by survivors of the epidemic of bubonic plague that scoured Europe, North Africa, India, and Asia in the mid–fourteenth century. That epidemic killed about a third of the people in Europe in less than ten years. It was later called the Black Death, but at the time, Europeans knew it simply as the Great Dying. It was one of many epidemics given similar terrifying names in different times and places.

An ancient fear returns

Until the twentieth century, infectious diseases—diseases caused by living things, usually microscopic, that invade the body—killed more human beings than war or famine. Often these diseases were simply an everyday hazard of life, slaying a few people here and there. Many infectious diseases, however, are also contagious (able to be spread from person to person by direct or indirect contact), and, at times in human history, these diseases have erupted in the terrifying bursts called epidemics. In an epidemic, the numbers of sick and dying rose rapidly until nearly everyone in a village or city was infected. People lived in constant fear that an infectious disease would kill them or wipe out their families.

Most people in industrialized countries no longer feel that fear. They have never lived through an epidemic. They may never have had an infectious disease worse than a cold or the flu. They believe that if they ever should catch a more serious infection, antibiotics or other weapons of modern medicine would cure it quickly. Epidemics like the one Agnolo di Tura described could never strike again, they think, except perhaps in some poverty-stricken country in a distant part of the world.

Growing numbers of scientists who study infectious diseases think such beliefs are dangerously misguided. Epidemics are not a thing of the past, nor are they always easy for doctors to control. They can strike any nation, rich or poor. Present-day conditions, ranging from a rapidly climbing world population to international jet travel, are setting the stage for epidemics that could once again make scenes like that pictured by Agnolo di Tura common all over the earth.

Deadly competition

Experts have come to believe that the risk of epidemic diseases is on the rise because of what they have learned about the microorganisms, or microscopic living things (sometimes also called microbes or germs), that cause those diseases and the ways these microbes interact with human beings. Both microorganisms and humans share the goals of all living things—to survive and reproduce their kind as effectively as possible. Microbes that cause human disease (which make up only a tiny fraction of the many kinds of bacteria, viruses, and other microorganisms that exist on Earth) must compete with humans to meet these goals. When either humans or microbes change their behavior, evolution favors those members of the other group that can respond to the change in a way that helps their survival and that of their offspring. When humans began to live together in cities, for instance, disease microbes that reached new victims through direct contact or through the air won an evolutionary advantage because the crowding allowed these germs to infect large numbers of people quickly.

People have one advantage in this competition: they can use their intelligence to find ways to avoid or destroy disease-causing microorganisms. Microbes, however, have a matching—perhaps more than matching—advantage in that they can reproduce much faster than humans. Bacteria, for instance, can produce a new generation every twenty minutes. Each time microbes reproduce, their genes (units of hereditary information) can undergo random changes, or mutations. Each mutation has the potential to give a microbe a winning characteristic, such as the power to resist an antibiotic. Humans evolve mutations that help them resist microorganisms, too, but the process takes much longer.

In spite of their reproductive advantage, microorganisms might not have caused so much damage to humanity if humans did not unknowingly help them. The circumstances that made history's Great Dyings possible have been set up primarily by changes in human behavior. Some current changes, experts think, are encouraging old epidemic diseases to return and new ones to invade large populations. Only careful planning and global cooperation among scientists, governments, and ordinary citizens can prevent the development of modern epidemics more deadly than any ever known before.

1

Death and Victory

FROM THE BEGINNING of human development, history—that is, people's behavior, both as individuals and in groups—has shaped epidemics. Epidemics, in turn, have shaped history. The outcome of wars, the rise and fall of empires, have often depended more on microbes than on rulers or armies. Microbiologist Hans Zinsser has written that epidemic disease "has decided more [military] campaigns than Caesar, Hannibal, Napoleon"[2] and all the other famous war leaders of history.

The birth of epidemics

Scientists who have studied the remains of early humans believe that these ancestors had infectious and contagious diseases. They seldom had epidemics, however, because they lived in small groups (a hundred people at most) and did not stay long in one place. Microbes therefore had little chance to infect, or invade the bodies of, large numbers of people at once.

Humans began encountering more disease-causing microorganisms when they started farming and domesticating animals about ten thousand years ago. Clearing land to make new fields exposed people to microbes that had formerly hidden in the forest. Irrigation ditches and wells were sources of standing water in which microbe-carrying mosquitoes could breed. Stored grain attracted rodents that carried still other germs. Each type of domestic animal had its own diseases, and some of these, in time, became able to infect humans. (This process also occurred with some diseases

Scientists believe that some diseases can be traced to human interaction with domesticated animals.

of the wild animals that were hunted by humans.) Scientists think measles came from dogs, influenza (flu) from birds and pigs, and tuberculosis from cattle, for instance. Throughout history, humans have probably caught more than two hundred kinds of diseases from their domestic animals.

Crowd diseases

Unlike their wandering ancestors, farmers lived in permanent settlements. Both garbage and population built up in such settlements, laying the groundwork for epidemics. However, epidemics did not become common until—about seven thousand years ago—humans began to pack themselves into cities of several thousand. City dwellers are constantly in contact with other people. Many are also exposed to human waste, leftover food, pests such as rats and mosquitoes, and other sources of microbes.

An epidemic can continue only as long as each sick person infects, on average, more than one other person, and this can happen most easily in crowds. Many diseases that cause epidemics are therefore called "crowd diseases." As infectious disease expert C. J. Peters writes:

> Put people close enough together in their slum or shantytown living conditions so that when one expires [breathes out] air, someone else inspires it [breathes it in], where they defecate in rivers where downstream others are getting their drinking

water and washing their clothes, and that's going to be just like compressing uranium to make an atomic bomb [in terms of starting an epidemic].[3]

Long-distance travel and trade, which developed along with cities, increased the risk of epidemics by accidentally bringing in microbes from distant places. Wars did the same thing. Microbes could be carried not only in the bodies of traders or invading soldiers but in their animals; their clothing, food, or other goods they carried; and pests that accompanied them, such as lice, fleas, and rats.

Types of germs that a group has never encountered are more likely to start epidemics within the group than familiar microbes because of the way the body's defense system against disease, the immune system, works. After people have recovered from an infectious disease, their immune systems usually develop defenses against the type of microbe that causes that disease. These defenses keep such persons from being reinfected by that type of microbe again for a long time, perhaps for their whole lives. When a group of people encounters a new type of disease-causing microbe, however, no one in the group has any immunity, or resistance, to it. The microbe can therefore spread quickly through the group.

Among the earliest epidemics of which historians have a detailed account is the Plague of Athens. Beginning in 430

One of the first recorded epidemics was the Plague of Athens, which began in 430 B.C. and killed up to one-third of the city's population.

B.C. and lasting several years, it killed a quarter to a third of the population of that ancient Greek city-state. "The bodies of dying men lay one upon another," wrote the historian Thucydides, who lived through the epidemic. "Half-dead creatures reeled about the streets and gathered round all the fountains in their longing for water."[4] Adding its disruption to that already caused by a war with the neighboring city-state of Sparta, this plague almost destroyed Athenian society. No modern disease has exactly the symptoms (signs of illness) Thucydides described, so no one may ever know for sure which microbe to blame for the disaster.

The Black Death

Plagues, as epidemics were often called, struck the ancient world regularly. None, however, was as terrible as the epidemic that swept through Europe in 1347, the one Agnolo di Tura wrote about: the Great Dying, or Black Death. This may have been the world's first pandemic, or epidemic that strikes much of the planet simultaneously. It raged in China and India at about the same time as in Europe.

The killer in this pandemic was the particular disease now called plague. It has two main forms, bubonic and pneumonic. Bubonic plague produces dark, swollen lumps called buboes under the skin, whereas pneumonic plague attacks the lungs. A bacterium named *Yersinia pestis* causes both forms of the illness. It lives in the guts of fleas that suck blood from rodents. When an infected flea bites a rat—or, occasionally, a human—it injects plague bacteria into the wound, causing bubonic plague. The pneumonic form spreads through the air in droplets from victims' coughing and sneezing.

Traveling with traders and warriors (for instance, in the food supplies that such groups carried), rats and their fleas spread bubonic plague through Asia and then into Europe. The European part of the Black Death pandemic began in Italian seaport cities, probably carried in by flea-ridden black rats aboard the ships of traders returning from the East. Once spread to humans, bubonic plague sometimes changed to the pneumonic form and spread even faster.

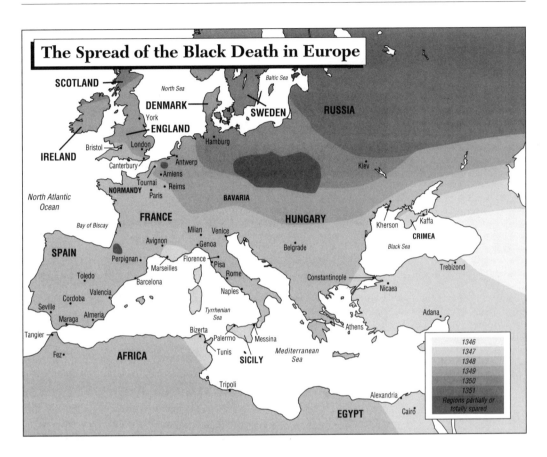

The Spread of the Black Death in Europe

SCOTLAND
North Sea
Baltic Sea
DENMARK
SWEDEN
RUSSIA
York
ENGLAND
Bristol
London
Hamburg
IRELAND
Antwerp
Kiev
Canterbury
Amiens
North Atlantic
Ocean
Tournai
Reims
NORMANDY
Paris
BAVARIA
FRANCE
HUNGARY
Bay of Biscay
Milan
Venice
Kherson
Kaffa
Avignon
Genoa
CRIMEA
SPAIN
Perpignan
Belgrade
Black Sea
Florence
Marseilles
Pisa
Trebizond
Toledo
Barcelona
Rome
Constantinople
Cordoba
Valencia
Naples
Nicaea
Seville
Almeria
Tyrrhenian
Sea
Adana
Maraga
Bizerta
Athens
Tangier
Palermo
Messina
Fez
Tunis
Mediterranean
AFRICA
SICILY
Sea
Tripoli
Alexandria
EGYPT
Cairo

| 1346 |
| 1347 |
| 1348 |
| 1349 |
| 1350 |
| 1351 |
| Regions partially or totally spared |

Like people stricken by epidemics in earlier times, many people who faced the Black Death believed that God had sent the plague as a punishment for their sins. Some spent their days in prayer or joined groups who wandered through the streets whipping themselves and each other, hoping to turn away God's wrath by punishing themselves. Others, feeling that they were going to die soon no matter what they did, began an endless round of feasting, dancing, and drinking. Still others turned their frustration and rage on "outsider" groups such as the Jews, massacring them by the hundreds.

"Flee quickly, go far, come back slowly"

People realized that the plague could be spread by contact with the sick, so many cities tried to keep sick people away. The Italian seaport of Venice, for instance, required arriving ships, crews, and goods to remain outside the city for forty days (*quaranti giorni*) to allow time for signs of plague to appear. The word *quarantine,* meaning isolation of sick people to stop the spread of disease, is derived from this restriction.

No one knew about the link between plague and rats or fleas, let alone bacteria. Most doctors thought that, like other epidemic diseases, the Black Death was caused by foul gas given off by decaying matter. (The name of another epidemic disease, malaria, means "bad air" in Italian.) They said people might escape the disease by purifying the air in their homes with flowers or other sweet-smelling substances. The only preventive measure that was likely to work, however, was the one summed up in an Italian proverb that translates, "Flee quickly, go far, come back slowly."[5] Even that would succeed only if neither the fleeing people nor the places they fled to already contained plague germs.

A woodcut depicts a bubonic plague victim pointing out the characteristic swelling under his arm to three attending physicians.

The Great Dying ended after less than a decade. Plague epidemics continued to sweep through Europe every ten years or so for the rest of the century, however. They reappeared at longer intervals until the early 1700s. Together these epidemics wiped out about 56 million Europeans, changing the continent's society forever. One casualty of the plague was the feudal system, in which peasants worked permanently, almost like slaves, on land owned by a noble. The system was already weakening by the fourteenth century, but the plague gave it its death blow by killing many of the peasant laborers. The remaining ones were so sought after that they could demand higher wages and more freedom.

Devastation in the Americas

Epidemics in the sixteenth and seventeenth centuries changed the Americas as completely as those in the fourteenth century had changed Europe. Before the first Europeans arrived in 1492, the natives of North and South America had seldom suffered epidemics. They had few domestic animals, so they had never developed the diseases that the farmers and herders of Europe, Africa, and Asia had caught from their beasts. They had not lived in cities as long as Europeans and therefore had not experienced many crowd diseases. They had encountered none of the microbes common in Europe, so their bodies were completely defenseless against these germs.

The guns and horses of the Spanish conquistadores may have frightened the American natives, but it was the invaders' unintended and invisible weapons, the disease microbes, that destroyed them. Hernán Cortés was able to conquer the fierce Aztecs of Tenochtitlán (now Mexico City) in 1521 with a mere handful of soldiers chiefly because of smallpox, a virus-caused disease that is often fatal and can leave its survivors blind or disfigured by the scars from its oozing rash. This disease, accidentally brought to Mexico by an infected slave from the Spanish settlement in Cuba a year earlier, killed nearly half of Tenochtitlán's occupants before the Spaniards even entered the city.

Hernán Cortés was able to defeat the Aztecs with a small number of soldiers due to the smallpox epidemic in Tenochtitlán.

Smallpox attacked the rest of the Aztec empire with equal ferocity. Toribio Motolinía, a Spanish priest, wrote that

in most provinces more than half the population died . . . in heaps, like bedbugs. Many others died of starvation, because, as they were all taken sick at once, they could not care for each other. . . . In many places . . . everyone in a house died, and, as it was impossible to bury the great number of dead, they pulled down the houses over them in order to check the stench [stop the bad smell] that rose from the dead bodies, so that their homes became their tombs.[6]

Smallpox was soon joined by measles, influenza, plague, and other European epidemic diseases. These illnesses, often carried ahead of the invaders by fleeing natives, destroyed one civilization after another throughout the Americas. Explorers such as Hernando de Soto, who visited the Mississippi River valley around 1540, sometimes found villages occupied only by the dead. Historians estimate that the Americas held about 100 million people before the Europeans arrived. That population was reduced by 90 to 95 percent over the next several centuries, mostly by epidemic diseases.

Imports from Africa

When Europeans settled in the Americas and began raising crops such as tobacco and sugarcane, they needed large numbers of workers to tend them. Because so many American natives had died, European plantation owners began importing slaves from Africa. Some of the slaves suffered from infectious diseases called malaria and yellow fever. American mosquitoes bit the slaves, picked up disease-causing microbes from their blood, and transferred these to Europeans and the remaining Native Americans with additional bites.

Malaria, a disease that destroys red blood cells, had existed in Europe (as well as in Africa, India, and China) at least since the days of the Roman Empire. Yellow fever, however, was new to Europeans as well as Native Americans. "Yellow jack," as it was nicknamed, caused frequent and deadly epidemics in the southern United States until the early twentieth century. Malaria, meanwhile, sapped the strength of frontier settlers in North America and plantation owners in the Caribbean.

Like plague and smallpox, malaria and yellow fever changed history. For instance, when the French emperor Napoleon sent an army of thirty-three thousand to reinforce France's claim to New Orleans and other land in North America and the Caribbean in 1802, twenty-nine thousand of the soldiers died of yellow fever. For this reason, among others, Napoleon concluded that his country's landholdings in the American tropics were impossible to defend. In 1803 he sold the immense tract of French-held land to the United States for a bargain price. Thus that young country more than doubled in size—partly thanks to yellow fever.

A nineteenth-century plague

In the nineteenth century, Europe developed a new plague of its own: cholera. This disease, caused by a comma-shaped bacterium called *Vibrio cholerae,* produces diarrhea and vomiting so severe that its victims can die in days or even hours from loss of water. Cholera spreads when germ-filled fluids from people with the disease get on others' hands or into drinking water and are swallowed.

Cholera has existed in India since ancient times. Traders and soldiers visiting the subcontinent exported the disease to China, Japan, North Africa, and the Middle East in the early nineteenth century, and by 1817 a cholera pandemic had begun. A second pandemic, in the 1830s, reached Europe and the Americas. A total of six cholera pandemics raced through the world as the century progressed. They spread mostly in the slums of the world's rapidly growing cities, where poor

The Industrial Revolution brought many workers together in crowded, filthy cities, paving the way for cholera epidemics in Europe and America.

people worked in the Industrial Revolution's new factories and lived in appalling conditions of crowding and filth.

By this time, however, doctors and health reformers were finally starting to have an effect on epidemics. Most still believed that epidemic diseases were caused by "bad air," but they no longer merely told people to avoid or disguise unpleasant smells. Instead, they began a campaign to remove the odors' sources: the rotting food, dead animals (and sometimes humans), unwashed clothing, and human and animal waste that filled streets and homes. They installed sewers and attempted to clean up prisons, hospitals, and slums. Where they were successful, the number of new cases of cholera and other epidemic diseases usually began to drop.

Disease detectives

Cleaning up slums did not always prevent cholera, however, and a few doctors wondered why. John Snow, a British physician who studied the disease in London during the third pandemic, published his most famous observations in 1854. In one London district, he noticed that people in some houses got cholera, but those in neighboring houses did not. By careful questioning, he learned that all the houses with cholera cases took their drinking water from a hand-operated pump on Broad Street. The healthy households got their water from other sources. Snow demanded that city officials remove the pump's handle so people could no longer use it. When they did so, cholera began to vanish from the area.

Snow later did larger studies that confirmed his guess that cholera was spread by polluted water. He and other nineteenth-century "disease detectives" established a new branch of medical science called epidemiology, which is the study of how diseases are spread and why they affect some people and not others.

Improvements in microscopes in the 1830s enabled researchers to study microorganisms dependably for the first time. Beginning about a decade after Snow's landmark work, a French chemist, Louis Pasteur, and a German physician, Robert Koch, used these tools to show what

French chemist Louis Pasteur linked microbes with decay and disease.

actually caused epidemic diseases. In the 1860s, Pasteur linked particular microbes to spoilage or decay in wine, meat, and other plant and animal products. He showed that microorganisms were common in the air, especially in places where large numbers of people, animals, and their waste could be found. Then, in the 1870s, he proved that certain germs were associated with, and probably caused, particular diseases found in silkworms, cattle, and humans. Robert Koch confirmed this germ theory of disease in 1882 by proving that a particular kind of bacterium caused tuberculosis, an epidemic disease that destroyed the lungs and sometimes other organs of many of Europe's poor.

Preventing epidemics

In addition to showing that microbes could cause sickness, Louis Pasteur helped to develop vaccination, a major tool for preventing epidemics. Vaccination puts killed or weakened disease-causing microbes into a person's body in a mixture called a vaccine. The vaccine stimulates the immune system to develop resistance to that type of microbe, just as infection by the natural microbe would, but it does not make the person ill.

A British country doctor named Edward Jenner had invented vaccination almost a century before Pasteur's work. Jenner noticed that dairymaids, who milked cows for a living, seldom suffered from smallpox. On questioning the women, he found that most had caught cowpox (vaccinia), a disease similar to smallpox but much milder, from the cows they handled. Jenner wondered whether deliberately giving someone cowpox could keep the person from getting smallpox.

In 1796, Jenner gave a boy cowpox by scratching material from a cowpox sore into his skin. Six weeks later, he scratched smallpox matter into the child's skin as well. The boy stayed healthy because the virus that causes cowpox is so closely related to the one that causes smallpox that an attack of cowpox makes a person immune (resistant) to both diseases. Word of Jenner's technique spread, and vaccination, as it came to be known, eventually wiped out smallpox in Europe.

In the early 1880s, Pasteur expanded Jenner's discovery by creating vaccines for rabies, anthrax (a serious epidemic disease of cattle and sheep that can also affect humans), and a form of cholera that affected chickens. Unlike Jenner's, Pasteur's vaccines contained microbes that had been deliberately weakened so that they could no longer cause disease. Later researchers made vaccines against other epidemic diseases.

In the late nineteenth and early twentieth centuries, scientists following the methods of Snow, Pasteur, and Koch identified most of the microorganisms that caused epidemic diseases and discovered how the illnesses spread.

Edward Jenner vaccinates a child. Jenner's discovery helped to eliminate smallpox in Europe.

For instance, they became able to see viruses, the tiniest of all microorganisms, and proved that these caused smallpox and some other epidemic diseases. They showed that the microorganisms that caused malaria, yellow fever, and certain other sicknesses were transmitted by the bite of mosquitoes or other insects. This fourth method of spreading infectious disease was added to the known ones of direct contact and via air, food, or water.

Armed with this new knowledge, health workers became able to prevent many epidemics by removing sources of infection or by vaccinating people. At the same time, improved nutrition, reduced crowding, and better living conditions strengthened people's immune systems and helped them resist disease. Epidemics therefore began to disappear from Europe and North America.

The end of epidemics?

Microbes were far from totally defeated, however. They reminded everyone of that in 1918, just as World War I was ending, when a pandemic of influenza swept the world. Most people think of "flu" as a fairly mild disease, but the form of influenza virus that caused this pandemic was a killer. It probably developed first in pigs in the American Midwest and then spread to people. (Ironically, even though the disease first appeared in the United States, it became known as the "Spanish flu" because an outbreak in Spain was the first to be widely publicized.) It produced the worst single epidemic in human history, killing at least 20 million people within a few months. Only half as many had died during the entire world war. The pandemic ended after about a year, as mysteriously as it had begun.

Amazingly, most people in Western nations quickly forgot the terror of the flu pandemic. They focused instead on sci-

German researcher Paul Ehrlich invented the first drug to combat a specific disease-causing microbe.

entific advancements to cure as well as prevent epidemic diseases. In 1909 a German researcher, Paul Ehrlich, had invented a drug to treat syphilis, a sexually transmitted epidemic disease. This was the first drug created to combat a particular disease-causing microbe. The sulfa (short for sulfanilamide) drugs, which killed several types of bacteria, were discovered in the 1930s. They were followed by penicillin and a host of other antibiotics around the time of World War II. (Produced naturally by a fungus, or mold, penicillin had been discovered in 1928 but could not be made in large quantities until the early 1940s.)

Thanks to vaccines, antibiotics, and advances such as new chemicals that killed disease-bearing insects, epidemics seemed well on the way to extinction by midcentury. Most people in developed countries probably would have agreed with then-U.S. surgeon general William H. Stewart when he said in 1967 that the United States could soon "close the book on epidemic diseases."[7] In 1979, as if to clinch human victory over infection, a massive, decade-long vaccination program sponsored by the World Health Organization (WHO) and the U.S. Centers for Disease Control and Prevention (CDC) succeeded in eradicating, or wiping out, naturally occurring smallpox worldwide. Surely, most people thought, the end of the rest of humanity's microscopic enemies would not be far behind.

They were very, very wrong.

2

Why Epidemics Are Returning

"ONE OF THE great lies of the twentieth century," writes Canadian science historian Andrew Nikiforuk, is that "antibiotics, vaccines and doctors have saved us from pestilence [epidemic disease]."[8] Far from being defeated, epidemics are making a powerful comeback today. Infectious disease, in fact, is the world's single most common cause of death. It is estimated to have accounted for 17 million of the 52 million deaths that occurred in 1995, for instance. Even in the United States, known for its medical technology, deaths from infectious diseases rose 58 percent between 1980 and 1992. By the late 1990s, infections were the third-largest killer of Americans, after heart disease and cancer.

Masses on the move

Many of the conditions that encourage modern epidemics are the same ones that spawned ancient plagues, but they now exist on an unprecedented scale. Perhaps the most important of these conditions is the rapid increase in the number and crowding of the world's people. If global population continues to grow at its present rate, it is expected to exceed 7 billion by the year 2020. Even more important from the standpoint of epidemics is the prediction that two-thirds of those people will live in cities with a population greater than 1 million.

As the world's population grows and cities become more crowded, the potential for epidemics increases.

The world already contains about fourteen megacities, each with a population of 10 million or more. Especially in the developing world, most people in these cities live in conditions as bad as or worse than those in the plague-stricken Middle Ages. About 1.2 billion people lack clean, safe drinking water. Furthermore, the immune systems of many poor people have been weakened by malnutrition, exposure to pollution, or sicknesses such as AIDS. They therefore have little power to resist epidemic disease.

Overcrowding and poverty also encourage epidemics indirectly by forcing people to seek new homes. The United Nations and the Worldwatch Institute estimated that in 1994 at least 110 million people in the world moved to another country. Another 30 million moved from the countryside to cities within their own country, and 23 million became refugees because of war or social unrest. Just as such people always have, today's migrants are likely to bring disease microbes with them and help to create fertile conditions for the microbes to grow. War refugees, for example, often must live in crowded camps with little food and no sanitation. When some family members (usually fathers) move to cities to look for work and leave others behind, families are broken up for long periods. The isolated members may turn to behaviors that encourage infectious disease, such as casual sex and use of injected drugs.

Changing the environment

Some migrants invade areas where few people have lived before. This is happening today in many developing countries, where people are cutting down rain forests for timber or to create farmland. Rain forests, with their great variety of plants and animals to infect, are the world's largest reservoirs of viruses except perhaps for the oceans. Settlers or workers in such places may encounter microbes that have seldom infected humans and unintentionally introduce these microorganisms to larger groups. Newly discovered infections such as Ebola fever and AIDS probably arose in this way, starting as animal diseases and then becoming able to affect humans. In the United States, Lyme disease (which can produce serious joint and heart damage if not treated) first became known in the 1960s and 1970s when growing eastern suburbs invaded what had been forest land. This move brought people into contact with deer and the tiny, insectlike deer ticks that transmit the disease.

Clearing land and setting up farms have always changed the environment in ways that can encourage the spread of disease microbes and their carriers. Modern technology

The deforestation and settlement of rain forests exposes people to disease-causing microorganisms in the native plants and animals.

adds to this effect. Cutting down forests, for instance, may change the numbers and distribution of plant and animal species, including those that carry diseases. In addition to ponds, open barrels, and irrigation ditches, pools of water in tin cans and discarded tires now provide places for mosquitoes to breed.

Trade and travel, too, can now spread disease-causing microbes to an extent never possible before. More than 500 million people cross international borders on commercial air flights each year. They—and any germs they might be carrying—can reach any part of the globe in a matter of hours. Food and live animals are also shipped all over the world, potentially carrying microbes with them. Infectious disease expert George J. Armelagos has written that rapid long-distance travel and trade are turning the planet into a "viral superhighway."[9] Bacteria and other microorganisms travel on the superhighway as well.

Some scientists suspect that technology is also encouraging epidemics more indirectly by creating or speeding up changes in the world's climate. Climate change or unusual weather may have played a role in several recent epidemics, including a 1991 cholera epidemic in Peru and an outbreak of pneumonic plague in India in 1994. Many scientists think the earth is heating up because human industry is increasing the amount of carbon dioxide gas in the atmosphere, thereby making the air hold in more of the sun's warmth (the so-called greenhouse effect). If the planet's temperature does rise, tropical diseases and their carriers, such as mosquitoes, might become able to spread into more temperate environments. Although scientists disagree about the level of danger, the United Nations Intergovernmental Panel on Climate Change predicted in a 1996 report that global warming "is likely to have wide-ranging and mostly adverse [harmful] impacts on human health, with significant loss of life."[10]

Deadly needles

Overconfidence in medical technology has opened the door to new epidemics by making governments think that expensive efforts such as vaccination programs or sanitation projects are no longer necessary. Sadder still, misuse of medical tools themselves is spreading some diseases. For instance, hypodermic syringes, or "shot needles," can become contaminated with blood containing the viruses that cause AIDS, hepatitis (a liver disease), or some twenty other serious illnesses. If reused without sterilization by high heat, contaminated needles may transmit those diseases to new victims.

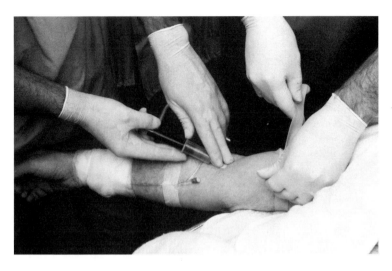

Some hypodermic syringes destroy themselves after one use, preventing contaminated needles from being reused and spreading disease.

In developed countries, contaminated hypodermics spread disease mostly among people addicted to injected drugs, who often share needles. Health care workers also sometimes catch diseases when they accidentally stick themselves with contaminated needles. The problem is far worse in developing countries, where clinics and hospitals frequently reuse unclean needles because of lack of money, training, or equipment. A 1998 World Health Organization (WHO) report claimed that 10 million people a year acquire fatal diseases from hypodermics.

Hypodermics meant to be discarded after a single use have existed since the late 1950s. Not all countries have them, however, and those that do may reuse them because they cannot afford to buy more needles. Hypodermics that destroy themselves after one use, making reuse impossible, were invented in the 1980s. They are more expensive than disposable or reusable hypodermics, though, and they have not become widely used. Until they do, contaminated needles will continue to be important disease carriers in many parts of the world. Contaminated blood transfusions present similar risks.

Antibiotic resistance

Overconfidence and misuse have produced another epidemic booster that is perhaps even more effective than contaminated hypodermics: antibiotic resistance. More than two dozen types of bacteria have become able to fight off at least one antibiotic. Some strains (subtypes) of three potentially deadly kinds can resist all of the hundred or so antibiotics now in existence. The WHO stated in 1994 that resistance is epidemic throughout the world. "We are living in the twilight of the antibiotic era,"[11] George Armelagos wrote in 1998.

Resistance to antibiotics was first reported in the 1940s, soon after the drugs came into use. It is a natural result of evolution. Antibiotics were first made from substances that molds or other living things had used to destroy bacteria for millions of years. During that time, by chance, some bacteria acquired genetic mutations that let them inactivate or otherwise resist the drugs. Low doses of antibiotics kill the weakest bacteria, but those that happen to have resistance genes survive the drugs, multiply, and pass the genes on to their offspring. The medications give resistant disease-causing microbes a further advantage by killing harmless bacteria that compete with them for resources.

Developing resistance may be more than a matter of luck. Experiments have shown that stress from the environment—such as the stress of being exposed to an antibiotic—can speed up the mutation rate in some bacteria. This increases the chances that resistance genes will appear. Furthermore, bacteria have several ways of sharing genes with other bacteria, even those of different species. Some genes can be passed between bacteria during a sexlike process called conjugation. Certain viruses that infect bacteria can also transfer genes from one type to another. Some bacteria vacuum up genetic material spilled out by others that are dead or dying. Resistance genes may happen to be among the ones exchanged in any of these ways.

Resistant bacteria are most likely to appear in places where antibiotics, many types

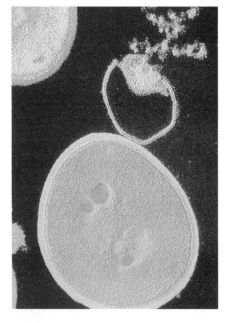

Antibiotics destroy the outer membrane of one staph bacterium while the one below it remains unaffected.

of bacteria, and human crowds can all be found. Such places include day care centers, nursing homes, and, above all, hospitals. The Centers for Disease Control and Prevention (CDC) estimates that more than 2 million Americans a year develop infections after they arrive in hospitals, a rate that has risen by 36 percent in the last twenty years. Antibiotic-resistant bacteria cause 70 percent of those infections.

Misuse of medicines

The more often bacteria are exposed to nonfatal doses of antibiotics, the more likely resistance is to develop. Widespread resistance is thus a direct result of antibiotic overuse and misuse—and these occur everywhere. For instance, although antibiotics have no effect on viral diseases such as colds or influenza, many people demand antibiotics for themselves or their children at the first sign of such illnesses, and doctors comply. "At least half the human use of antibiotics in the United States is unnecessary or inappropriate," claims Stuart Levy of Tufts University School of Medicine in Boston. "Either antibiotics are not indicated at all, or the wrong antibiotic is prescribed, or it's the wrong dosage or wrong duration [length of time during which the patient takes the drug]."[12] Furthermore, people often quit taking the medicines as soon as they stop feeling sick, even if their doctor has prescribed a longer treatment. This means that they do not receive enough drug to kill all the disease-causing bacteria in their bodies, and the hardier germs survive.

People consume some antibiotics without even knowing it. Low doses of these drugs are often given to healthy cattle, chickens, or other food animals to prevent disease and help the animals gain weight. (The energy that untreated animals would need to fight off bacteria, the theory goes, will be used to make more flesh in treated ones.) About 40 percent of the antibiotics made in the United States, in fact, are given to animals. Crop plants also are sometimes treated with antibacterial compounds. Traces of antibiotics remain in foods made from these plants and animals, further encouraging resistance.

Inventive evolution

Development of antibiotic resistance is just one way that microbial evolution can spark new epidemics. Disease-causing viruses and other microorganisms can evolve resistance to drugs that attack them, much as bacteria do with antibiotics. Microbes can also evolve the ability to withstand disinfectants, live at higher or lower temperatures than before, or survive for longer periods outside a living body. "Think of microbes as swimming in a great stew in your nose, your throat, your intestines. This shuttling of genes is going on everywhere,"[13] says Richard Krause of the Fogerty International Center, part of the National Institutes of Health (NIH) in Bethesda, Maryland.

Viruses can evolve what amounts to resistance to vaccines as well as to drugs. A vaccine primes the immune system to react to chemicals on the surface of a particular type of microbe. Some viruses, such as the ones that cause AIDS and influenza, frequently mutate in ways that change

'That's one antibiotic-resistant virus.'

Reprinted by permission of *The Spectator*, London.

those surface chemicals. The result is "new" microbes that the immune system can no longer recognize or protect the body against. In effect, the virus puts on a disguise so that its appearance no longer matches the one on the "wanted posters" that the vaccine has passed out.

Disease-causing microbes sometimes evolve new methods of attack as well as defense. These can include ways to spread more easily. For instance, the form of *Yersinia pestis* that causes bubonic plague can spread only through the bite of rat fleas, but the form that causes pneumonic plague can spread through the air. After repeated contacts with humans, microbes that infect animals may develop the power to infect people as well. As previously mentioned, this is thought to have happened in ancient times with the viruses that cause measles and smallpox and during the twentieth century with the virus that causes AIDS. Finally, a microbe that once was harmless or caused only minor illness may gain a mutation that enables it to do more serious damage. This happened when one strain of a bacterium called *Escherichia coli* (or *E. coli*), which normally lives in the human intestine without causing disease, developed the power to produce severe food poisoning in the early 1990s.

When the ancient powers of microbial evolution and human foolishness combine with the new ones of modern technology, they produce possibilities for the spread of epidemic diseases that seem limitless. No wonder, then, that infectious disease is reappearing in both old and new forms. According to a 1996 estimate, at least twenty-nine previously unknown infectious diseases have been identified since 1973. Furthermore, at least twenty familiar diseases thought to have been defeated by medical science have reappeared, often in forms more powerful than the original ones. Many experts feel that, unless major changes are made in world health care, a deadly pandemic of some kind is almost sure to happen before long.

3

Emerging Epidemics

MANY EPIDEMIC DISEASES that threaten the world today never infected humans on a large scale, or perhaps at all, until the late twentieth century. Some of these "emerging diseases" are caused by microorganisms that have only recently developed the power to infect humans or make them sick. Other emerging diseases have greatly increased the area over which they spread or the number of people they infect.

AIDS: collapsing defenses

AIDS is by far the best known of emerging diseases. Most scientists believe that this illness is caused by a virus called HIV (human immunodeficiency virus), which is very similar to viruses that cause AIDS-like illnesses in certain African monkeys and apes. Many AIDS experts suspect that an ancestor virus made the leap from these animals to humans when people in central or west Africa ate infected animals or perhaps were bitten or scratched. The first modern AIDS cases seem to have appeared around the middle of the twentieth century, but infection may have occurred now and then for hundreds of years before that.

Health workers first suspected the existence of this new disease around 1980, when doctors in New York, San Francisco, and Los Angeles reported that growing numbers of drug abusers and homosexual men were dying of formerly rare types of pneumonia, cancer, and other ailments. Tests showed that the sufferers' immune systems were devastated, leaving them open to infections that healthy immune

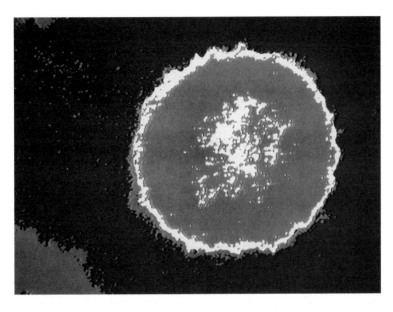

A microscopic view of HIV, the virus that causes AIDS.

systems could fight off. This immune collapse was soon recognized as a disease in its own right and given the name AIDS. In 1982, separate teams of French and American researchers found convincing evidence that its cause was the virus that became known as HIV, which infects and destroys certain cells in the immune system.

Scientists learned that HIV can spread only by contact with blood, semen, or other body fluids, which usually occurs during sex or through transfusion or injection of infected blood. AIDS is thus much harder to catch than diseases caused by microbes that can spread by casual contact, such as a handshake, or through the air. On the other hand, most people infected with HIV remain seemingly healthy, yet able to infect others, for years before showing symptoms of AIDS. This fact, combined with certain changes in human behavior, has allowed AIDS to become a worldwide epidemic.

Behavior creates a pandemic

The behavior changes that have helped AIDS spread became common in the 1970s. Some occurred in Africa. The population of many African countries rose rapidly, which forced some families to seek timber or farmland in what had been virgin forest. This increased their chances of coming into contact with infected monkeys. In the cities, social disruption caused by war and unemployment brought increases in prostitution, sexual promiscuity, and abuse of injected drugs. Hypodermic needles and blood transfusions contaminated with HIV meanwhile infected people who visited hospitals and clinics.

Behavior changes outside Africa gave the disease a further boost. In addition to promiscuous heterosexual behavior, some homosexual men in large cities of the United States and Western Europe also began living openly promiscuous lifestyles. This potentially allowed a single person carrying HIV to infect hundreds of sexual partners. Abuse of injected drugs also increased in some cities. At the same time, jets took people and blood products from one part of the globe to another more quickly than ever before. All these activities helped to turn AIDS into a pandemic.

A man dying of AIDS lies in a hospital in Ivory Coast, Africa, his body ravaged by the disease.

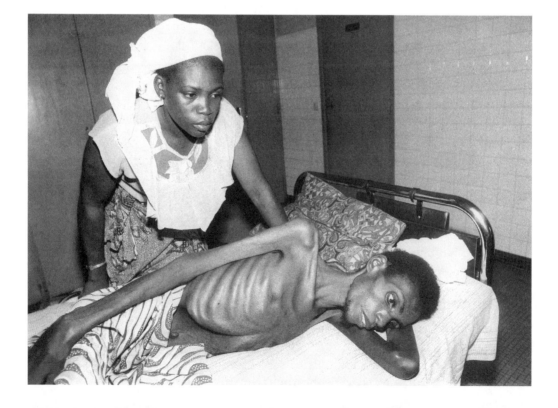

The United Nations AIDS program estimated that 33.4 million of the world's people were living with AIDS in 1998. Two and a half million people died from the disease that year, and 5.8 million new victims became infected. Educational campaigns, screening of blood supplies, and new treatments were starting to control AIDS in developed nations during the late 1990s, but the AIDS pandemic was increasingly devastating the developing world. There the disease has orphaned millions of children and depleted a whole generation of adult workers, threatening to destroy already shaky economies. "AIDS is reversing decades of progress [in] improving the quality of life in developing countries,"[14] said Martha Ainsworth, a senior economist of the World Bank, in 1997.

Ebola: a bloody death

Ebola fever is far less widespread than AIDS—it is so far known to have affected only a few thousand people worldwide—but it is perhaps the most dramatically deadly of emerging diseases. It makes blood leak from every organ and body opening and kills up to 90 percent of its victims within a few days. No wonder Ebola or fictional diseases based on it have been featured in movies, TV shows, and books.

Ebola was first identified in 1976, although, like AIDS, it may have existed long before then. It, too, is caused by a virus. Even more surely than AIDS, it came from the rain forests of central Africa. The Ebola virus probably lives there in some type of animal, but scientists do not yet know which kind.

A 1976 photo of the Ebola virus from Zaire.

The first known outbreaks (small epidemics) of Ebola occurred in 1976. One happened in the southern Sudan (east central Africa). Two months later, it was followed by a second outbreak near the Ebola River in the central African country of Zaire. In each case the disease infected about three hundred people, killed 60 to 90 percent of them, then died away.

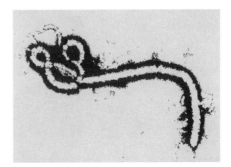

Little else was heard of Ebola until 1995, when a new outbreak struck Kikwit, a town of about half a million people in Zaire. Like the 1976 outbreaks, the one in Kikwit centered on a hospital. It began on April 9, when a thirty-five-year-old laboratory technician named Kimfumu came to Kikwit General Hospital with a high fever, headache, and diarrhea. Doctors operated on him twice to try to find out what was wrong, but he died three days after he arrived. By then, some doctors and nurses who had taken part in the operations had become sick as well. Blood-contaminated hypodermics, bedding, and other medical supplies spread the disease to additional hospital employees and to patients. Sick people took it into the surrounding community.

The Kikwit hospital asked the WHO for help on May 7. The WHO, in turn, sent samples of sick people's blood to the CDC, which identified the Ebola virus in them. An international medical team rushed to Kikwit, where they helped local health workers isolate the sick and bury the dead. They also brought clean needles, gloves, masks, and other supplies. Some team members traveled to nearby villages to trace those with whom the sick people had had

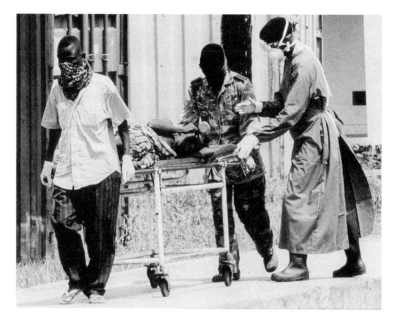

A patient infected with the Ebola virus is transported in Kikwit in 1995.

Relatives of Ebola patients cover their noses and mouths to protect themselves from infection as they wait outside the Kikwit hospital for news. In fact, Ebola is spread not by air but by contact with infected blood.

contact and, if necessary, isolate them, too. These actions probably helped to limit the size of the outbreak. Like the earlier outbreaks, however, the one in Kikwit ended on its own in less than two months. It infected 316 people and killed 245 of them.

Ebola may die out so quickly because, unlike AIDS, it kills people before they can spread the disease to many others. "If you look at it from an evolutionary point of view, you can sort out the 95 percent of disease organisms that aren't a major threat [to humanity] from the 5 percent that are," says infectious disease expert Paul Ewald of Amherst College in Massachusetts. "Ebola really isn't one of those 5 percent."[15]

Hantavirus: drowning on dry land

Anyone who thinks that emerging diseases come only from distant rain forests should consider the events that began on May 14, 1993. On that day, while riding in a car with his parents, an athletic young man in New Mexico suddenly began to gasp for breath. He had recently been sick with what he thought was the flu. He was rushed to the Indian Medical Center in Gallup, but within hours he was dead. His lungs were filled with fluid. In effect, he had drowned on dry land.

Alert New Mexico medical examiners noticed that this unusual death was similar to five others that had recently occurred in the Four Corners region, where the states of Arizona, Utah, Colorado, and New Mexico meet. On May 18, they notified the CDC that an outbreak of a new disease might be in progress and asked for the agency's help.

As cases of the deadly illness continued to appear, the CDC sent a team of epidemiologists to New Mexico. They talked to sick people and their families, collected samples of their blood, and sent these back to the agency's headquarters in Atlanta, Georgia. When the samples were tested for signs of microbes that matched those in the CDC's large collection, the only ones that seemed similar were a family of viruses called hantaviruses. These viruses seemed unlikely culprits, since they had been found mostly in Asia and had never been known to affect the lungs. Even so, less than a month after the young athlete's death, the CDC confirmed that the cause of all the Four Corners illnesses was a seemingly new type of hantavirus. They called it Sin Nombre (Spanish for "no name") or Muerto Canyon virus.

Hantaviruses normally infect rodents, which they do not make ill. Humans become infected when they inhale dust containing dried saliva, urine, or droppings from the animals. On June 18, after many tests, scientists from the

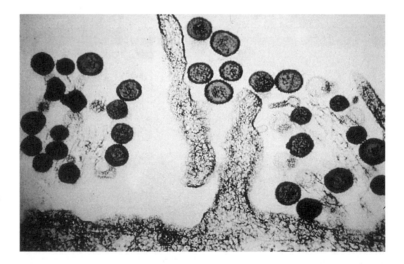

The hantavirus usually lives in rodents but it can pass to and fatally infect humans.

CDC and the Indian Health Service identified the rodent carrier of the Sin Nombre virus. It proved to be the deer mouse, a very common animal that lives in open areas and little-used buildings but sometimes invades people's homes in search of food.

Unusually heavy rains and warm temperatures the previous winter had produced huge crops of pine nuts and other foods, and this in turn had caused a deer mouse population explosion in the spring. The scientists suspected that this increase in the number of deer mice had triggered the sudden outbreak of hantavirus-caused illness around Four Corners. Fortunately the number of mice dropped again in the summer, and the virus outbreak also ended. Its final total was eighteen cases and eleven deaths.

The real mystery about hantaviruses in the United States is why they sicken so few people. The Sin Nombre virus proved to be very widespread among deer mice, which suggested that this "new" microbe in fact had probably lived in North America for centuries. Deer mice, in turn, are found almost everywhere in the United States. Similarly, Seoul virus, a hantavirus that causes bleeding in the kidneys, has been found in rats that live in American city slums. Millions of people thus must be exposed to these viruses. By late 1995, however, hantavirus infections—about half of them fatal—had been identified in only 111 Americans, spread among twenty-three states. Most hantavirus infections probably are never identified as such, but this number still seems surprisingly small. Perhaps the few people who do become sick have a gene that makes them unusually vulnerable to the viruses.

E. coli and others: contaminated food

Illness caused by hantaviruses may be fairly rare, but the same is not true of another group of emerging diseases, which are spread through food. Food-borne diseases have always been common in the developing world. During most of the twentieth century, however, they have been unusual in industrialized countries. That may be changing. In the late 1990s, for instance, food-borne diseases were known to have sickened a minimum of 6.5 million Americans a year and killed about 525. Because these illnesses are often not reported to authorities, the true numbers may be much higher. Some groups say that microbes in food cause up to 81.4 million illnesses and 9,000 deaths in the United States each year.

The emerging food-borne disease that has gained the most attention is caused by a bacterium called *Escherichia coli*. *E. coli* is usually a harmless inhabitant of human intestines. However, a strain of these bacteria called O157:H7, first identified in 1982, causes serious illness. It was blamed for a 1993 epidemic around Seattle, Washington, in which five hundred people, mostly children, became sick and at least four died. All proved to have eaten undercooked, contaminated hamburgers at Jack-in-the-Box fast-food outlets. *E. coli* O157:H7 also caused a food poisoning outbreak among children who drank apple juice bottled by Odwalla, a California company, in 1996. CDC researchers estimated in 1997 that this new *E. coli* strain sickens twenty thousand or more Americans a year and kills up to five hundred. It causes similar problems in other developed countries.

A plate of O157:H7 E. coli *colonies, which cause illness and sometimes death.*

Other new or changed microorganisms have also spawned epidemics of food-borne disease. *Campylobacter,* a bacterium found in 63 percent of raw chickens tested, has been blamed for between 2 and 8 million cases of food poisoning and between 200 and 800 deaths in the United States each year. Another microorganism, *Cyclospora,* contaminated raspberries and strawberries from Guatemala and sickened 1,012 people in the United States and Canada in 1996. Bacteria belonging to a genus called *Salmonella,* which can live in undercooked poultry and eggs, cause an estimated 2 to 4 million further illnesses in the United States yearly. In all, at least 25 new microbes or new strains of older ones that can cause food-borne diseases have been identified since 1975.

Mass-produced epidemics

Experts believe that the chief reasons for the rise of food-borne diseases are changes in farming and ranching methods that increase the spread of disease-causing microbes. First, tens of thousands of chickens or other meat animals are often crowded together on huge "factory farms." Crowding encourages epidemics among animals, just as it does among people. It also increases the chances that carcasses and products such as eggs and milk will be contaminated by excrement.

Some groups maintain that crowded, unsanitary conditions in slaughterhouses increase the chances that microbe-carrying meat will be sold. For instance, Gail Eisnitz, author of a 1997 book called *Slaughterhouse,* claims that "deadly, contaminated meat is just pouring out of . . . [slaughtering] plants, and I have the documentation to prove it."[16] For example, Eisnitz says, poultry inspectors used to be able to stop slaughterhouse production if they found any contamination, such as feces or open sores, on slaughtered birds. Eisnitz claims, however, that since the early 1980s, most inspection has been done by slaughterhouse workers. The workers' employers strongly discourage them from "stopping the line" except when birds are very obviously diseased.

Critics claim that current meat-processing procedures allow contaminated meat to pass through slaughterhouses and infect the public.

Fruits and vegetables, too, particularly those imported from developing countries, may pick up germs from polluted water or from human or animal excrement used as fertilizer. All these raw foods can introduce microorganisms into machinery used to process them. Because many foods are mass processed, a single contaminated machine can spread microbes to large quantities of food. Restaurant workers and home consumers often make the problem worse by not cooking and storing foods safely.

Food sold in the United States is supposed to be inspected by the federal Food and Drug Administration (FDA) and other agencies, but critics say that inspection procedures are often inadequate. In 1998, *New York Times* reporters Christopher Drew and Pam Belluck called American food inspection "a patchwork of weak state agencies and a lumbering federal bureaucracy . . . focused more on reacting to [food-borne illness] outbreaks than preventing them."[17] Similarly, a 1998 report from the U.S. General Accounting Office stated that neither the FDA nor the Department of Agriculture had the personnel nor the legislative power to enforce inspection standards for imported food.

Creutzfeldt-Jakob disease: mad cows and mad people

Surely the most frightening of emerging food-borne diseases is one thought to be caused, not merely by a new strain of bacteria or virus, but by a completely new type of disease-causing agent. The agent, called a prion, is a deformed version of a normal brain protein. It can somehow change healthy molecules of the same protein to its own shape. Thus, in effect, it reproduces, even though it contains no genes. When prions multiply, they destroy nerve cells and turn the brain into a sponge full of microscopic holes, eventually causing death. Brain diseases thought to be caused by prions affect sheep, cattle, mink, and occasionally other animals. Human prion diseases also exist but have been thought to be very rare. Prion diseases are spread by eating infected brain or nerve tissue.

Few people had heard of prions until March 1996, when the British government confirmed reports that ten young Britons had recently died of a seemingly new form of a prion-associated brain disorder called Creutzfeldt-Jakob disease (CJD). The story made headlines because of the possibility that they had caught the disease by eating beef from cattle that suffered from another prion disease, bovine spongiform encephalopathy (BSE) or "mad cow disease." Beef cuts sometimes include nerve tissue, such as parts of the spinal cord.

BSE had become widespread among British cattle in the late 1980s, affecting about 160,000 of them by 1996. Researchers believed that the cattle first developed the illness because they had been fed the ground-up remains, including brains, of sheep that suffered from still another prion disease. The government banned the feeding of sheep and

'My only consolation is that by eating us, they're killing themselves.'

cattle remains to cattle in 1989, which should have stopped new infections. Because BSE, like AIDS, shows no symptoms for years after infection, however, apparently healthy cattle infected by prions could still have gotten into Britain's beef supply.

The British government played down possible danger: "It isn't the cows that are mad, it's the people,"[18] said health secretary Stephen Dorrell. Still, the 1996 headlines produced a tremendous health scare. Beef consumption in the whole European Union dropped by 30 percent, and many countries stopped importing British beef or cattle. To calm everyone's fears, the government had to order the slaughter and burning of thirty-seven thousand seemingly healthy cattle that had been alive before 1989 and therefore might have eaten prion-contaminated feed.

In time the panic died down, and by the end of 1998, only a handful of further CJD cases had appeared. Concern remains, however. Two studies published in 1997 strengthened the evidence that BSE in cattle and the new form of CJD in humans are the same illness. The possibility remains that more—perhaps many more—CJD cases will appear in future years. Furthermore, although BSE has never been seen in North American cattle, researchers say there is no reason why it could not appear and spread on that continent. "The only thing that stands between us and an epidemic" of CJD, Robert Roher, director of molecular virology at the Veterans Administration Medical Center in Baltimore, told *Time* magazine in 1997, "is . . . luck."[19]

HIV, Ebola virus, hantavirus, *E. coli* O157:H7, and the prions that cause Creutzfeldt-Jakob disease are just a few of the seemingly new disease-causing agents that have come to medical attention since the 1970s. So far, except for HIV and perhaps *E. coli,* these emerging agents have affected only small numbers of people. The history of the AIDS pandemic, however, shows how quickly that can change.

4

Old Killers Strike Back

EMERGING DISEASES MAY be frightening, but many experts think that the worst risk of devastating new epidemics comes instead from ancient illnesses, once thought to be defeated, that are now returning. "We have untreatable infections in our hospitals here in the U.S. right now," said Mitchell Cohen of the CDC's National Center for Infectious Diseases in 1996. "We know another flu pandemic is coming. To me, these things are of much more concern than something terrible from the jungle."[20]

Plague: panic in India

One killer that staged a comeback during the 1990s was the most feared infectious disease of all: the plague. An epidemic of pneumonic plague, the most dangerous form of the disease, appeared in Surat, a city of about 2 million people on India's west coast, in September 1994. Some epidemiologists think the epidemic started because of an increase in rats (and therefore rat fleas) following unusually heavy flooding during the monsoon (storm) season. With half of Surat's people living in shacks or on sidewalks with no sewers or running water, the plague bacteria found an ideal environment in which to multiply.

Fortunately, plague can be cured by antibiotics if it is caught early enough, and the Surat outbreak was apparently caused by a fairly weak strain of bacteria. Isolating and treating patients therefore brought the epidemic under

A young man infected with the pneumonic plague is brought to a hospital in Surat, India, by family members.

control in a little over a month. Before it stopped, however, the Surat epidemic sickened thousands and killed at least three hundred people. Carried by citizens fleeing in panic, the disease even spread to India's capital, New Delhi, some six hundred miles (one thousand kilometers) away.

The Indian plague showed that the social and economic effects of a modern epidemic can reach far beyond the sickness and death caused by the disease itself. Airports in a number of countries, for instance, increased health screening or quarantining of passengers on flights from India. A few nations banned all flights to or from the stricken country. Furthermore, while the epidemic was at its height, India lost at least $2 billion in product sales and stock market investments, because the epidemic had caused some foreign countries to cut off imports from India (for fear of transporting plague bacteria) and to curtail investments in companies there.

Cholera: a new pandemic

Cholera, the disease that led John Snow to lay the foundations of epidemiology more than 150 years ago, is another epidemic sickness that never really died. No cholera pandemics occurred in the first half of the twentieth century, so many scientists thought that improvements in sanitation had largely controlled the disease. In 1961, however, a new strain of the cholera bacterium appeared in Indonesia. It began a pandemic that is still under way on six continents. Cholera caused 2.5 million deaths worldwide in 1997, according to a WHO estimate.

The cholera pandemic made headlines in the West in 1991, when the disease reached the Americas for the first time in a hundred years. The American epidemic started in January in Peru, perhaps because a ship from Asia dumped a ballast load of infected water into Callao harbor. "We had a powder keg ready to explode," said CDC medical epidemiologist Fred Angulo, "an entire continent in which the sanitation and public water supplies and everything was primed for transmission of this organism."[21] Peru, Ecuador, and Colombia were the most heavily affected, but the epidemic eventually spread to most parts of both continents. It made at least 300,000 people sick and caused about 4,000 deaths before subsiding toward the end of the year. Cases of cholera were still occurring in many Latin American countries in the late 1990s.

The new cholera pandemic has helped scientists learn important facts about the disease, some helpful and some disturbing. The most heartening finding is that a simple, inexpensive treatment called oral rehydration therapy can reduce the disease's death rate from 20 percent to 1 percent. The treatment helps people's bodies maintain their fluid levels until their immune systems have time to destroy the cholera bacteria.

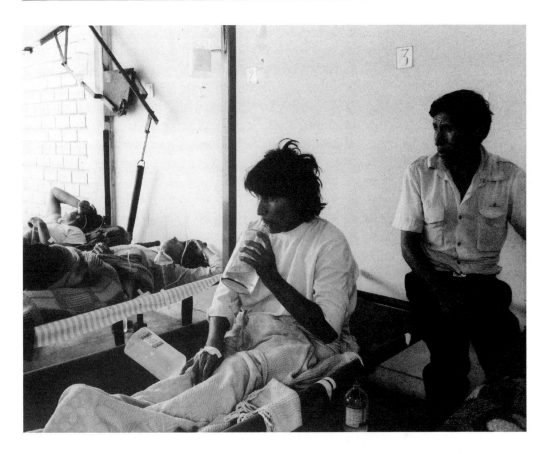

More frightening discoveries relate to the cause of the disease. One is that cholera bacteria live on billions of tiny shrimplike creatures that float in seawater. The bacteria survive in this natural reservoir between human epidemics and can be carried great distances by ocean currents. This means that, although cholera epidemics may be controlled, the disease will probably never be eradicated. A warming climate, furthermore, may push cholera pandemics into high gear by increasing the number of these sea creatures. Cholera expert Rita Colwell thinks the Latin American epidemic spread so quickly because ocean warming produced by the weather pattern called El Niño had this effect.

Cholera-infected patients await treatment at a hospital in Lima, Peru.

Strep and staph: resistant to everything

Old epidemic diseases have returned in developed as well as developing countries. In the summer of 1994,

British newspapers announced that six people in Gloucestershire had died of what sounded like a new and terrible illness: necrotizing fasciitis (decaying skin), which some papers called "flesh-eating strep." The disease has also appeared in the United States. This infection can start in a tiny cut and progress through an arm or leg almost fast enough to watch, dissolving tissue as it goes. Unless treated promptly with antibiotics, it can cause loss of a limb or death within hours.

"Flesh-eating strep" is indeed terrible, but it is not really new. It is a rare form of infection by a common bacterium called streptococcus type A. The truly frightening fact about streptococcus and an even more common and dangerous wound-infection bacterium, *Staphylococcus aureus,* is not their power to cause these occasional fearsome infections but their growing ability to cause less intense but still serious illnesses that do not respond to antibiotics.

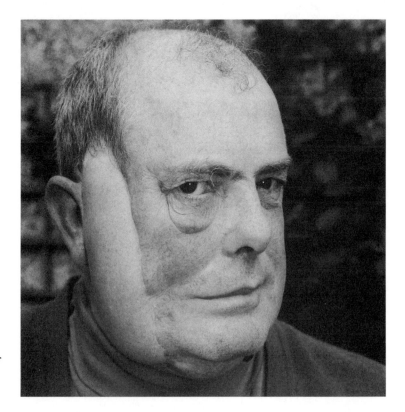

A survivor of necrotizing fasciitis. He underwent six operations to cut away the diseased portion of his face and replace it with healthy tissue.

Both strep and staph, as these bacteria are called for short, turned hospitals into death traps until the mid–nineteenth century, when doctors began learning how to keep them out of wounds and surgical incisions. Antibiotics later reduced these germs' powers further. Today, however, strep and staph are once again major hospital dangers—thanks to advances in medical care. Extremely sick people can be kept alive in intensive care units by machines connected to them through tubes. Staph, strep, and other microbes use those tubes as highways into the people's weakened bodies.

In recent years, staph and strep have developed resistance to most antibiotics by exchanging genes with other types of bacteria found in hospitals. One of these types, *Enterococcus faecalis,* now possesses a gene for resistance to an expensive "last-resort" antibiotic called vancomycin. Doctors' greatest fear is that staph and strep will acquire this gene. If they do, these bacteria could produce infections that essentially cannot be stopped. In fact, four cases of vancomycin-resistant streptococcus infection were reported in early 1998.

Influenza: Hong Kong "bird flu"

As with emerging diseases, the old diseases that cause spectacular outbreaks, such as plague, cholera, and flesh-eating strep, tend to grab headlines while far worse killers lurk almost unnoticed in the background. One potential slayer is influenza, an illness that most people in developed countries think of as a mere wintertime nuisance. Although no new flu epidemic as deadly as the 1918 one has yet appeared, pandemics in 1957 and 1968 reminded scientists that this disease can be a serious problem.

Just as plague bacteria survive on wild rodents and cholera bacteria on sea creatures, influenza viruses live in wild ducks and other migrating waterbirds. The viruses can also infect domestic ducks, geese, and chickens. Some strains of bird flu virus can infect pigs, as can strains of flu virus that infect humans. Scientists believe that most new strains of flu virus are created when bird and human

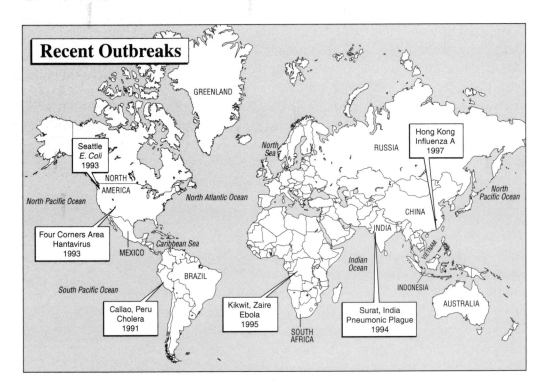

Recent Outbreaks

GREENLAND

Seattle
E. Coli
1993

NORTH
AMERICA

North Pacific Ocean

North Atlantic Ocean

Four Corners Area
Hantavirus
1993

MEXICO

Caribbean Sea

BRAZIL

South Pacific Ocean

Callao, Peru
Cholera
1991

North
Sea

RUSSIA

Hong Kong
Influenza A
1997

North
Pacific Ocean

CHINA

INDIA

VIETNAM

Indian
Ocean

INDONESIA

AUSTRALIA

Kikwit, Zaire
Ebola
1995

SOUTH
AFRICA

Surat, India
Pneumonic Plague
1994

viruses mix in pigs and exchange genes. This happens most often in Asia, where people, chickens, ducks, and pigs all live close together on farms.

Health experts have come to believe that the only way to prevent a new flu pandemic is to keep a worldwide watch for emerging strains of flu virus. A network of doctors constantly tests pigs, chickens, and human flu patients to see what strain of virus they carry. They report seemingly new strains to the CDC or other research centers. In June 1997 one member of this network, Wilina Lim of the Department of Health in Hong Kong (a territory on China's southern coast), informed the CDC that such a strain had caused the death of a three-year-old boy a month before. Seventeen more flu cases caused by the same strain appeared in November and December, and five of those stricken died. By then the virus was killing thousands of chickens in the territory's farms and live-animal markets.

After testing many blood samples from both birds and people, researchers determined that the responsible virus

Workers on a farm in Hong Kong collect garbage bags filled with chickens that were euthanized following the 1997 flu outbreak.

was indeed a new strain. They called it influenza A (H5N1). Unlike previously known strains, this one appeared to have spread directly from birds to people. To prevent a possible human pandemic, Hong Kong health officials ordered the slaughter of all the territory's domestic chickens, ducks, and geese, some 1.3 million birds, on December 28. Some critics doubted that such drastic action was necessary, but Kennedy Shortridge, an American flu virus expert who lives in Hong Kong, told *Discover* magazine, "I think

Hong Kong made the right decision"[22] to avert a pandemic. Because of either the chicken slaughter or the fact that H5N1 did not spread easily from person to person, no further cases of flu caused by that strain of virus appeared. The world was lucky—this time.

Malaria: a quiet killer

A microbe almost as changeable as the flu virus, and much more deadly on a regular basis, causes malaria, a quiet killer that produces even more yearly deaths than AIDS. Malaria, which is spread by the bite of certain mosquitoes, can kill as quickly as plague or cholera. Alternatively, it can weaken a person through a lifetime of repeated attacks. Since ancient times it has decimated armies and sapped the strength of nations around the world. Some estimates state that malaria killed half the people who ever lived.

In 1957, at the height of Western medical optimism, the WHO launched a campaign to eradicate malaria worldwide. It planned to do this mostly by killing the mosquitoes that carried the disease, using DDT and other powerful insecticides that had been developed during World War II. The program made the number of malaria cases drop tremendously for a decade or so. Then, however, financially strapped countries decided that mosquito control programs were no longer needed and cut back funding for them. At the same time, people began clearing more rain forest land and created new breeding places for mosquitoes. Widespread use of insecticides to fight pests on farm crops helped mosquitoes evolve resistance to the chemicals, just as overuse of antibiotics produced resistance in bacteria. The malaria microbes themselves also developed resistance to new drugs used to treat the disease. As a result of all these factors, malaria has rebounded. The number of cases worldwide quadrupled between 1992 and 1997.

Today, malaria affects almost 40 percent of the world's people and causes nearly 3 million deaths a year. It is the world's most widespread mosquito-borne illness. Yet because it tends to be a constant feature of life rather than producing suddenly rising numbers of cases—and, probably, because it affects few people in wealthy Western nations (90 percent of malaria cases are in Africa)—malaria prevention efforts have received relatively little international funding. One African doctor complained in 1997, "Westerners think only of HIV. HIV is horrible, of course. But it is malaria that keeps Africa down."[23] Some researchers think that in the future, global warming may bring malaria back to the West, where it was once common. If that happens, the fight against this quiet killer may finally gain the funding and personnel it needs.

Tuberculosis: a global emergency

Perhaps the greatest returning killer of all is tuberculosis (TB), which some estimates claim destroys more lives each year than any other infectious disease in the world. The WHO declared TB a global emergency in 1993. The organization estimated in 1995 that 1.7 billion of the world's

A tuberculosis patient in Hanoi, Vietnam, receives treatment from his doctor.

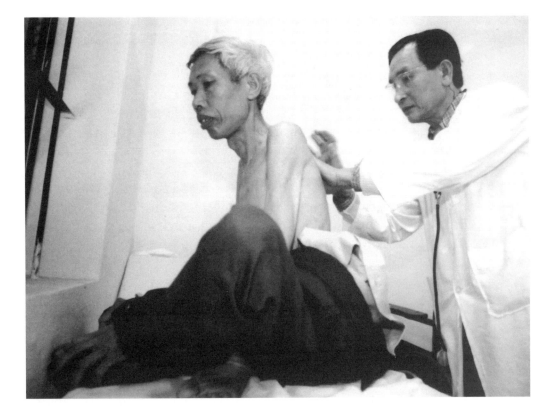

An African man with TB sits in an overcrowded prison in Rwanda. Crowding, malnutrition, and immune systems weakened by AIDS have contributed to a sharp rise in TB cases.

people (two-thirds of them in Asia) were infected with the disease and about 20 million were severely ill. The WHO claimed that TB caused 2.9 million deaths in 1997.

Caused by a bacterium, tuberculosis spreads through the air in droplets from coughs and sneezes. It causes little or no illness in 90 percent of the people it infects, but it can devastate those whose immune systems are weakened by malnutrition or other diseases. Because of its easy spread from person to person and its preference for people already in bad health, tuberculosis is a classic "crowd disease." Signs of it have been found in a three-thousand-year-old Egyptian mummy, but it became a widespread killer only in the packed city slums of the nineteenth century.

Thanks partly to antibiotics and partly to improved nutrition and living conditions, the numbers of tuberculosis cases and deaths fell sharply in the second half of the twentieth century. In the 1990s, however, TB made a comeback, increasing by 30 percent in parts of Western

Europe and by 20 percent in the United States. The number of cases in some African countries quadrupled.

As with malaria and other infectious diseases, TB's return has been spurred by a blend of medical pridefulness, which assumed that spending money on monitoring and treating the illness was no longer necessary, and the continuing existence of the poverty and unhealthy living conditions that foster it. Another booster is the HIV/AIDS epidemic, which has weakened the immune systems of millions and made them easy targets for the tuberculosis bacterium. "TB is like a shadow of AIDS"[24] because so many people with AIDS also develop TB, says Thavisakdi Banrungtrakul of the Thai National TB Program.

Worst of all, just like staph, strep, and other bacteria, many strains of the tuberculosis bacterium have become resistant to antibiotics. A 1998 study reported that one out of every six TB strains tested in thirty-five countries resists at least one drug. Two percent resist more than four drugs. The WHO estimated in 1997 that some 50 million people worldwide are infected with drug-resistant strains, which kill 50 to 80 percent of their victims.

Resistance has become widespread mostly because many tuberculosis victims do not complete their antibiotic treatment, even though the drugs are cheap and easily available. People must take several pills a day for at least six months in order to be fully cured, but many stop taking the drugs after a month or so when they start to feel better. This allows resistant TB bacteria to survive.

Even more than occasional spectacular outbreaks, the tremendous number of ongoing deaths from diseases like malaria and tuberculosis reminds humanity that epidemics never really died. The microbes that cause them simply retreated while they developed new strategies and weapons. Some of these may be more powerful than any countermeasures that human science has created.

5

Epidemics
in a Test Tube

NATURAL EPIDEMICS ARE scary enough. Today, however, people have come to fear a type of disaster that in some ways seems even worse: an epidemic caused by bacteria or viruses that either escape accidentally from a laboratory or are unleashed deliberately as an act of warfare or terrorism. Small-scale incidents of these kinds have already happened, and many experts think that larger ones may soon follow.

Close brushes with disaster

Individuals have certainly died from epidemic diseases accidentally acquired from laboratories. For instance, the last recorded death from smallpox took place in 1978, after the disease had been eradicated in nature. At that time, stocks of the smallpox virus were kept at several laboratories in different parts of the world. The virus somehow escaped from a laboratory at the University of Birmingham in Britain and fatally infected Janet Parker, a medical photographer working on the floor above. Two years later, partly because of the Parker accident, the WHO ordered all stocks of the virus to be destroyed except for those kept for research purposes at the CDC in the United States and the Research Institute of Viral Preparations in Moscow.

The closest brush the United States has had with an epidemic caused by accidental release of microorganisms occurred in late 1989 and early 1990 in Reston, Virginia, a town about twenty miles from Washington, D.C. It started when newly imported monkeys began dying in the quarantine facility of Hazelton Research Products, which sold animals to medical research laboratories. The sick monkeys showed bleeding and other symptoms like those of Ebola fever. Company veterinarians thought they had simian hemorrhagic fever (SHF), a similar but unrelated monkey disease.

To confirm this guess, Dan Dalgard, Hazelton's chief veterinarian, sent some blood from the monkeys to scientists at the United States Army Medical Research Institute of Infectious Diseases (USAMRIID) at Fort Detrick, Maryland. USAMRIID is a sort of military version of the CDC, concerned primarily with the protection of soldiers rather than civilians. When USAMRIID researchers Peter Jahrling and Tom Geisbert looked at the monkey blood with an electron microscope, they saw SHF virus, as they had expected. To their horror, however, they also saw the looping shape of what looked like the Ebola virus. They were puzzled as well as frightened because the infected monkeys had come from the Philippines, islands south of Asia, and Ebola had never been reported outside of Africa.

Jahrling and Geisbert took their electron micrographs to C. J. Peters, then head of USAMRIID's Disease Assessment

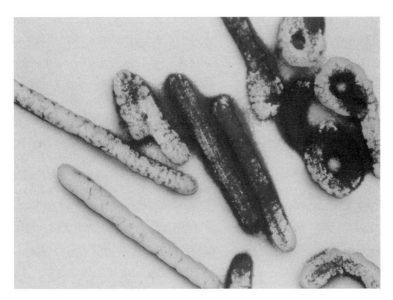

The Ebola virus. Samples of blood from monkeys infected with simian hemorrhagic fever in Reston, Virginia, also proved to contain the Ebola virus.

Division, on November 27. Peters ordered other tests, which confirmed that the virus was a strain of Ebola. On November 29, fearing a possible human outbreak of the deadly disease, Peters consulted with Joe McCormick, then chief of the Special Pathogens (disease-causing microorganisms) branch of the CDC. He also talked to Dalgard, Virginia state health department officials, and other experts. The group agreed that, as long as the disease was confined to monkeys, USAMRIID would handle it. The CDC and Virginia health authorities would deal with human cases if they appeared.

The first sick monkeys had all come from a single room at the Hazelton facility. Dalgard had had all the monkeys in that room euthanized soon after the illness broke out, but the disease nonetheless spread to a nearby room. This suggested the frightening possibility that, unlike the African strains of Ebola, this one could spread through the air. On December 1, at Dalgard's request, a group from USAMRIID gave fatal injections to all the monkeys in the second room as well.

An epidemic that didn't happen

The health team feared that a human epidemic was starting when an animal handler at Hazelton began vomiting and feeling weak and feverish on December 5. Fortunately the man recovered quickly, and tests found no trace of the Ebola virus in his blood. Meanwhile, however, the disease was still spreading among the monkeys. On the same day the animal handler fell ill, USAMRIID and the owners of Hazelton reluctantly agreed that all monkeys in the quarantine facility must be killed and the building completely decontaminated. The USAMRIID team spent three days euthanizing the monkeys. They then sealed the building and filled it with a gas capable of killing any virus left inside.

The threat was still not entirely over. In January 1990 a new shipment of monkeys from the same Philippine supplier also began dying of Ebola, and in mid-February a Hazelton lab worker cut his finger while operating on one of the dead monkeys. The man's blood showed signs of infection by the Ebola virus a few days later. Still, although CDC and USAMRIID scientists watched him carefully for weeks, he never became sick.

Later tests revealed that several other Hazelton workers had also been infected by the Reston strain of Ebola virus at some time, but they, too, had failed to become ill. For reasons still not entirely understood, the strain of Ebola in the Reston monkeys apparently could not cause disease in humans, even though it could infect them. In spite of USAMRIID's prompt action, only this fact may have kept the Reston incident from turning into a disaster.

Signs of biological warfare

Another accidental release of disease-causing microbes did produce a human epidemic. The epidemic, which took place in the Russian city of Sverdlovsk (now Ekaterinburg), caused at least sixty-four deaths and had implications that reached far beyond this small number of fatalities. On April 2, 1979, ninety-four people in Sverdlovsk suddenly became ill with anthrax, a bacteria-caused disease that usually affects sheep and cattle but can also kill humans. Russian government officials at first blamed the outbreak on contaminated meat. In 1992, however, Russian president Boris Yeltsin admitted that it had been due to an airborne leak of anthrax spores, a seedlike form of the bacteria that is very difficult to destroy. The spores had come from a nearby plant where they were being prepared for possible use in biological warfare.

Biological warfare is not a completely modern invention. People occasionally tried it even before they knew that epidemic disease was caused by microorganisms. A kind of biological warfare, in fact, may have helped to launch the "Black Death" epidemic of the Middle Ages. In 1346, Tatar (Asian) soldiers besieging the city of Kaffa (now Feodosiya), a trading port on the Black Sea, were stricken with plague and had to give up the siege. Before leaving, the surviving Tatars catapulted some of their diseased comrades' corpses over the city walls. Whether spread by the corpses or by the fleas on the rats accompanying the army, the sickness soon entered Kaffa. Among

Doctors treat a plague patient in the Middle Ages. The Black Death may have gotten a foothold in Europe because soldiers attacking the busy trading port of Kaffa catapulted diseased corpses over the city walls.

those who fled the city as a result were traders from the Italian city of Genoa. When they sailed for home, they took the plague with them.

Kaffa was just the beginning. Several times during their takeover of the Americas, Europeans gave Indians blankets that had been used by people with smallpox, knowing that the blankets would probably spread the disease to them. Similarly, Indians suffering from smallpox sometimes visited trading posts and forts in the hope of passing the illness to the Europeans there.

Only in the twentieth century, however, did biological warfare become an organized military activity. During

World War I, Norwegian police found a bottle containing two sugar cubes in the luggage of a suspected German spy. The cubes proved to be laced with anthrax spores, suggesting that the Germans were planning to use biological agents in the war as well as the poison gases they were already employing. The United States, Germany, and Japan all prepared biological weapons during World War II, and Japan actually used them in China in the 1930s and 1940s. United States military forces conducted extensive tests of such weapons, releasing supposedly harmless bacteria in or over cities such as San Francisco and New York, during the 1950s and 1960s. Several people are alleged to have died of illnesses resulting from these tests.

A secret program

In spite of the aforementioned incidents, the idea of biological warfare has seemed so horrible that most nations have formally promised not to use it. Along with chemical warfare, biological warfare was forbidden by the Geneva Protocol in 1925. A second treaty outlawing the stockpiling or use of biological weapons, the Biological Weapons Convention, was established in 1972. By 1996, a total of 137 countries had signed it, including the United States and the former Soviet Union.

Some countries lived up to their promises better than others. President Richard Nixon ended biological weapons research in the United States in 1969. He also ordered all facilities for producing such weapons to be dismantled. The Soviet Union, seeing this as a chance to gain an advantage in the cold war, secretly stepped up its own biological warfare program. High-ranking Russian scientists who defected in 1989 and 1992 told British and American intelligence agents that at its height, the Soviet program had involved dozens of plants and laboratories. It had employed more than thirty thousand workers and stockpiled hundreds of tons of weapons. The Sverdlovsk plant from which the anthrax spores leaked in 1979 was part of that program.

Although the Soviet Union has since collapsed, these defectors and others suspect that at least part of Russia's

Workers seal Iraqi rockets for destruction after the Persian Gulf War. The rockets were reportedly filled with the chemical nerve agent sarin. Both chemical and biological weapons are outlawed, but some countries nonetheless have them.

biological warfare research continues. Furthermore, some of the Soviet program's former scientists—and perhaps some of its weapons as well—may be enriching similar programs in other countries. In the late 1990s, U.S. government agencies claimed that as many as seventeen nations were known or strongly suspected to have biological warfare programs. These include Russia, China, North Korea, Israel, Iran, Iraq, and Libya. The Iraqi government has admitted to making weapons containing anthrax and other deadly microbes during the Persian Gulf War in 1991. When asked in a 1998 interview whether biological weapons would be used in the future, Kanatjan Alibekov, one of the Russian defectors, answered, "That's not a matter of if; that's a matter of when."[25]

Disease weapons

Among diseases that might be spread by biological weapons, anthrax not only was a Soviet favorite but remains the most likely choice for others. Anthrax bacteria are easy to obtain (spores can be found in the soil of any pasture where infected animals have grazed) and grow. Their spores are both hard to kill and easy to spread in an aerosol spray. Antibiotics can cure anthrax in its early stages, but the disease is hard to identify at that time because its first symptoms are like those of influenza and other common illnesses. Finally, anthrax is deadly: If untreated, it kills about ninety percent of the people it infects.

Other diseases likely to be used in biological warfare are plague and smallpox. Like anthrax bacteria, the microbes that cause these illnesses are sturdy, easy to spread, and deadly. After smallpox was eradicated and stocks of the virus that caused the disease were confined to only two laboratories, the Soviet Union realized that the world's population would be completely defenseless against the disease once everyone's vaccinations wore off. It therefore used its stock of virus to make biological weapons. Russia probably still possesses secret caches of smallpox virus, and other countries may as well.

As if these natural diseases were not bad enough, some countries may be trying to use genetic engineering to create resistant microbes or to combine the deadliest characteristics from several types. For instance, Kanatjan Alibekov has claimed that the Russians tried to combine genes from the smallpox and Ebola viruses.

Terrorist attacks

Governments are not the only ones that might use epidemic diseases as weapons. Unlike nuclear bombs, biological weapons are so easy and inexpensive to prepare and use that they might be employed by small terrorist groups or even individuals. Deadly microbes can be obtained from nature or from laboratories that stock them for the use of researchers. Information on growing and spreading them is available in books or on the Internet. For these reasons, biological weapons have been called "the poor man's atomic bomb."[26]

An incident in the United States in 1995 showed how easily terrorists could get the raw material for a biological attack. Using nothing more than a faked letterhead, an Ohio laboratory technician named Larry Harris ordered a supply of plague bacteria from the American Type Culture Collection, a respected biological supply house then located in

Rockville, Maryland. Luckily, remarks he made during a phone call made the company suspicious, and they alerted authorities. Police arrested Harris and seized the bacteria, which had been delivered to his home. Harris was later convicted of mail fraud, and requirements for obtaining dangerous microorganisms were tightened considerably the following year. A clever group, however, might still find ways around them.

Although no proven biological terrorist attack has yet occurred, some groups have clearly considered such attacks. For instance, Japanese police discovered that a religious cult called Aum Shinrikyo (Supreme Truth), which killed twelve people and injured more than five thousand on March 20, 1995, by releasing a nerve gas called sarin into the Tokyo subway system, was also attempting to prepare biological weapons. In 1997, an envelope of powder that the anonymous senders claimed was anthrax spores arrived at the world headquarters of the Jewish service organization B'nai B'rith in Washington, D.C. Fortunately, the powder proved to be harmless. Similar envelopes later sent to abortion clinics and other targets have also all been hoaxes—so far. The day may come, however, when such a threat turns out to be real.

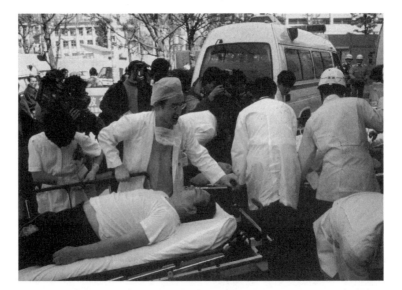

Victims of the Aum Shinrikyo nerve gas attack on the Tokyo subway system are rushed to the hospital.

Whether launched by an enemy government or a terrorist group, a biological attack could have devastating effects. The U.S. Office of Technology Assessment calculated that a crop-duster plane spraying 100 kilograms (220 pounds) of anthrax spores over Washington, D.C., could cause up to 3 million deaths. Similar spores spewed from the tailpipe of a car traveling around New York City might kill five or six million. Such an epidemic, furthermore, would almost surely overwhelm the medical system and cause panic, followed by social and economic collapse. Michael Osterholm, an epidemiologist in the Minnesota Department of Health, says that an epidemic of something like smallpox produced by a biological attack would create "the closest thing to a living hell we've probably ever known."[27]

Preparing for the unthinkable

The possibility of biological warfare or terrorist attack drew a lot of attention during the late 1990s, and developed countries' budgets for defense against it were increased considerably. In 1998, for instance, the United States Congress added $1 billion to the yearly $3.5 billion already devoted to development of defenses against chemical and biological warfare. The military also began immunizing all soldiers, especially those sent to the Middle East, against anthrax in March of that year. This was the first routine vaccination of U.S. forces against a possible biological warfare agent.

Because of these and other stepped-up activities, Secretary of Defense William S. Cohen said in a 1998 interview that, in his opinion, the United States was less vulnerable to biological attack than most other countries. Critics, however, insist that far more must be done, especially to protect against an attack on civilians. Michael Osterholm complains, for example:

> The beliefs of much of our governmental system . . . is that somehow rushing in, in space suits, with sirens, will deal with the bioterrorism problem. . . . It won't happen. It's going to be at the emergency room level, in the medical care

A 1998 photo shows a U.S. soldier in Kuwait receiving the anthrax vaccine.

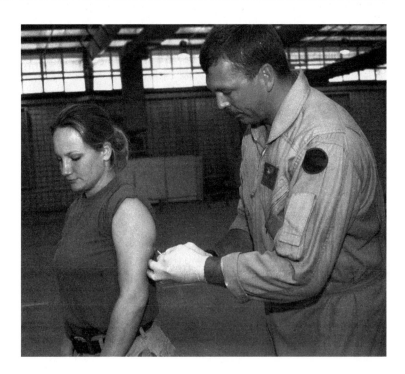

area, in the health departments, in our vaccines, in our antibiotics. If we don't have those, we have nothing to prepare for bioterrorism.[28]

In response to such criticisms, the U.S. government began a $42.6 million Domestic Preparedness Program, the largest civil defense initiative since the cold war, in 1997. The program aims to train local personnel to deal with a possible biological attack and provide a network whereby they can alert the CDC or other agencies of suspicious outbreaks. By 1999, 120 cities were participating in it.

While countries struggle to develop defenses against biological weapons, some scientists, such as Harvard molecular biologist Matthew Meselson, place their chief hope in the possibility that the world's moral disgust with such weapons will ultimately discourage governments or terrorist groups from using them. After all, says Meselson, "These are weapons that threaten any organized society. . . . It's the protection of our whole human species that we're talking about here."[29]

6

Tracking and Controlling Epidemics

W HEN AN EPIDEMIC strikes, the leaders of the attack against it are likely to be infectious disease experts from national or international organizations such as the CDC and the WHO. These highly trained men and women risk their lives to track and control epidemics, whether they are in Africa nursing a patient with Ebola or working in a protective "blue suit" in a high-tech laboratory filled with vials of deadly viruses. "We have to be prepared to do anything—clean floors, take samples [of blood and other body fluids], care for patients," says the CDC's Pierre Rollin, who went to Zaire when Ebola broke out there in 1995. "Conditions are very hard in the field . . . [sometimes including] no running water, no electricity, no clean needles. If you get into trouble, you cannot dial 911."[30]

CDC to the rescue

In the United States, the national agency with chief responsibility for handling civilian epidemics is the CDC. Epidemics are the specific focus of the CDC's National Center for Infectious Diseases (NCID), where about one thousand of the agency's seven thousand employees work. (The CDC also studies other threats to health, such as cancer, heart disease, and even violence.) The NCID works to

71

prevent epidemics through vaccination and education programs as well as to control them.

When state health authorities detect a suspicious outbreak and ask NCID for help, the agency sends a team from its Epidemic Intelligence Service. The teams call these assignments epi-aids. NCID handles up to 120 epi-aids a year, some in American states and some in foreign countries. "If there is a bad epidemic anywhere, from Minneapolis to Hong Kong, local people want the CDC there,"[31] says John Bartlett, chief of the infectious diseases unit at Johns Hopkins Medical School in Baltimore, Maryland.

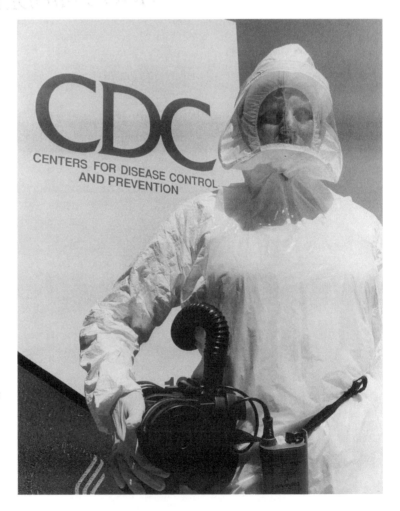

A CDC employee at the agency's headquarters in Atlanta models a protective suit worn by doctors working on the Ebola outbreak in Kikwit, Zaire.

A CDC team's main jobs on an epi-aid are to identify the microbe causing the outbreak and discover its source. To do these things, team members question sick people and their families, friends, and other contacts. They ask where the people have traveled recently, what they have eaten and drunk, what animals or animal products they might have encountered, and so on. They search the people's environment for signs of animals, insects, contaminated food or water, or other possible sources of disease. In addition to this detective work, they help local health workers treat sick people safely. They also provide education and other measures to help stop the epidemic's spread.

The strange world of BL-4

With the people's or their families' permission, CDC scientists on an epi-aid take samples of blood, tissue, or other substances from those sickened or killed by an epidemic and send them to the agency's headquarters in Atlanta. There, other scientists try to identify microbes in the samples by matching them with those in NCID's extensive collection. If the scientists cannot find actual microbes, they can sometimes identify the germs indirectly by testing for immune system products called antibodies, which are different for each type of microbe. Alternatively, they may use genetic engineering techniques to isolate some of the microbes' genes.

CDC laboratories are divided into levels according to the seriousness of the illnesses the microbes in them cause and whether there are treatments or vaccines for the sicknesses. Viruses that cause the common cold, for instance, might be studied in Biocontainment Level 1 (BL-1). BL-4, by contrast, is reserved for the deadliest and most uncontrollable microorganisms, such as the Ebola virus.

The BL-4 lab at the CDC is one of only two in the United States (the other is at USAMRIID) and about ten in the world. It is a place as alien as the moon. The lab must be entered through a series of chambers like the air locks on a space ship. Its ventilation system sucks air inward whenever a door is opened so that no microbes can blow

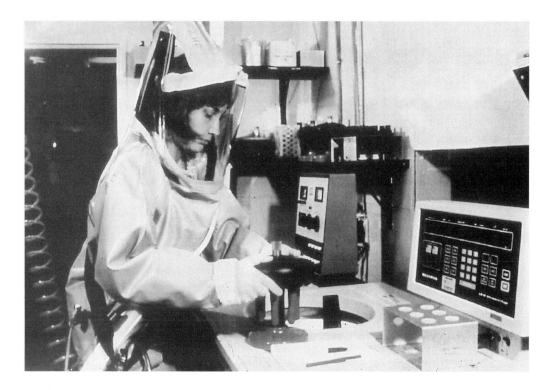

Protected by a maximum containment suit, a microbiologist studies a deadly virus in the BL-4 lab at the CDC.

outside. Before going into the lab, scientists must take off their own clothes and put on outfits like the ones surgeons wear in operating rooms. Over these they pull space-suit-like "blue suits," complete with hoses that provide a separate air supply. (CDC scientist David Bressler describes a blue suit as "claustrophobic, hot, and sweaty."[32]) When the scientists leave the lab, they must take a chemical decontamination shower while still in their suits. They then take another, standard shower before putting on their street clothes.

The WHO: international coordinator

Some other developed countries have national organizations similar to the CDC. In Germany, for instance, the Robert Koch Institute has served this function since 1996. If countries lack effective national disease control agencies, however, local authorities are likely to call on international agencies, especially the World Health Organization, if an epidemic starts. Today, the WHO's Division for

Emerging and Other Communicable Diseases Surveillance and Control, established in late 1995, handles the international equivalent of epi-aids. Besides helping to trace outbreaks and provide advice and medical supplies, it coordinates the work of other health and relief agencies.

Perhaps the WHO's greatest contributions to world health are its programs to prevent epidemics through widespread vaccination. The WHO sponsored the vaccination program that eradicated natural smallpox in the late 1970s. In 1974, furthermore, the organization launched a program to immunize all children against six other deadly infectious diseases: tuberculosis, diphtheria, tetanus, whooping cough, polio, and measles. By 1996, WHO-trained workers had vaccinated almost eighty percent of the world's children and were credited with saving at least 3 million lives a year. The program was expected to eradicate polio

A 1967 photo shows a WHO doctor vaccinating a baby in Turkey.

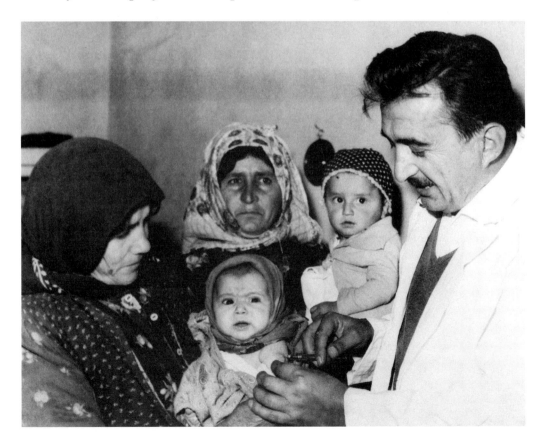

from the earth by the year 2000. The WHO, like the CDC, also attempts to prevent epidemics through education and training campaigns.

Finally, the WHO and other international health agencies, working with national agencies such as the CDC, track epidemics through global surveillance networks such as the one that identified the new strain of virus causing the "bird flu" in Hong Kong in 1997. Such networks are especially important for following microbes that change frequently, as the influenza virus does. The WHO and the CDC have jointly set up eight flu virus surveillance sites in China alone.

Preventing epidemics

In the mid-1990s, the CDC, the WHO, and similar agencies found themselves hard pressed to find enough money to do their work. Reporter Laurie Garrett claimed in 1996 that Dustin Hoffman's pay for starring in *Outbreak,* a movie about an Ebola-like illness, was greater than the combined annual budgets for NCID and the United Nations AIDS/HIV program. The widely publicized disease outbreaks of the first half of the decade, such as the Indian plague epidemic and the African Ebola outbreak, had put a dent in public and government complacency about infectious disease, however, and funding began to increase. As a result, there were signs that the world's power to prevent and control epidemics was starting to improve as the twenty-first century neared.

Some promising discoveries have come from basic research on disease-causing microbes. Geneticists have now decoded the genomes (complete collections of genes) of the bacteria that cause tuberculosis and syphilis. This information provides potential targets for new drugs and vaccines.

New vaccines against several major epidemic diseases are being tested in animals or humans. Several malaria and cholera vaccines, including some created by genetic engineering, are undergoing widespread human testing, and a vaccine against Lyme disease was approved for sale in the

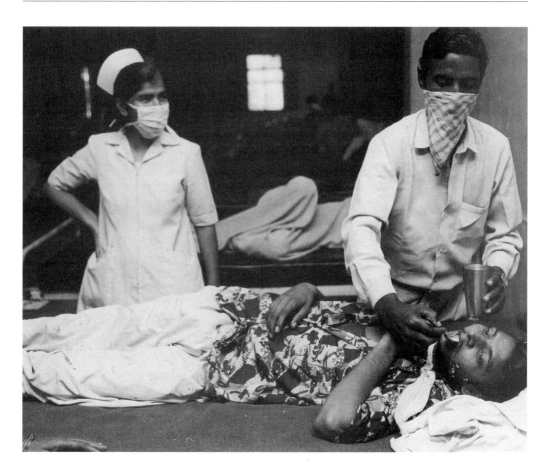

United States in 1998. USAMRIID announced in late 1997 that it had created an anti-Ebola vaccine that worked in guinea pigs. Improvements in existing vaccines, such as an influenza vaccine that can be given in a nasal spray rather than by injection, are also being tested. Efforts to create a vaccine for AIDS have so far been frustrating, but they continue.

A plague victim in New Delhi, India. As a result of the widely publicized plague outbreak, funding for infectious disease research began to increase.

On a more basic level, some scientists are rethinking the way vaccines are designed. Infectious disease expert Paul Ewald believes that scientists can encourage disease-causing microbes to evolve in ways that make them less virulent (able to cause serious illness and death) by making vaccines that target only the most virulent strains of such organisms rather than all strains. Such vaccines would slow the spread of the dangerous strains while allowing milder forms to survive. The mild microbes would then compete with the remaining virulent ones and perhaps eventually eliminate them. Alternatively, people could be "vaccinated" with antibiotic-susceptible, harmless bacteria that would compete with resistant ones. This approach is already showing success in baby chickens on factory farms. Still another new approach is shown in a malaria vaccine that, instead of preventing people from catching the disease, prevents them from infecting mosquitoes that bite them and thus passing it on.

Public education campaigns are also helping to prevent epidemics. For example, cholera expert Rita Colwell has shown people in Bangladesh how to protect themselves against cholera by filtering water through several layers of sari cloth, which is available to even the poorest families. Filtering through four layers of cloth, Colwell says, can remove 99 percent of cholera bacteria from contaminated water. If the filter is rinsed (with filtered water) and dried in the sun, it can be used repeatedly.

Predicting and tracking epidemics

When epidemics cannot be prevented, new technology may help scientists predict and track them. Photos taken by space satellites, for instance, can show subtle changes in environmental features, such as temperature, sea level, and vegetation patterns, that seem to be associated with outbreaks of particular diseases. The U.S. National Air and Space Administration (NASA) encouraged this use of satellites by forming the Center for Health Applications of Aerospace Related Technologies (CHAART) in the mid-1990s. Among other things, CHAART helped Rita Colwell discover that seasonal epidemics of cholera occur in Bangladesh soon after sea levels rise, making ocean water back up into rivers. Information like this can help health workers prepare for and perhaps limit or prevent epidemics.

The key to keeping a small outbreak from turning into a full-scale epidemic, most experts agree, is surveillance networks that provide rapid communication among local, national, and international health officials and scientists. Such

networks are the best safeguard against biological warfare attacks as well as natural
epidemics. By early 1998, eight national disease surveillance programs had been established in the United States. In 1995, fifteen
European countries formed a loose-knit organization called the Charter Group to help scientists exchange information about infectious
disease and track down outbreaks.

Not surprisingly, the Internet and the World
Wide Web play a major part in international
disease surveillance networks. In 1993, for
example, the WHO and the Federation of
American Scientists established a computer
conferencing system called ProMED (Program
to Monitor Emerging Diseases). ProMED allows its members—infectious disease experts, government health officials, doctors,
and other health professionals from more than
115 countries—to share information about
disease outbreaks via the Internet.

Modern communication allows scientists to share information quickly and track and treat epidemics effectively.

Treating epidemics

Better treatment may be able to control epidemics once
they do break out. Some improvements result from better
methods of giving existing drugs or other treatments. For
instance, even though drug-resistant strains of tuberculosis
bacteria have developed, cheap drugs presently in use can
still cure most TB cases if taken for the full time required.
A treatment system called Directly Observed Treatment,
Short Course (DOTS), helps to make sure that this happens. With DOTS, health care workers or family members
personally watch a sick person take the drugs every day
during the six-month treatment period. In China, where
about a quarter of the world's TB cases can be found,
DOTS has raised the cure rate from less than fifty percent
to more than ninety percent. In 1997, WHO director general Hiroshi Nakajima called DOTS "the biggest health
breakthrough of this decade."[33]

To combat germs that have become resistant to present-day drugs, drug companies are starting to develop new antibiotics and other antimicrobial drugs. Some experimental antibiotics are new versions of old drugs such as penicillin and vancomycin. Others, however, attack microbes in completely different ways. For instance, a group of antibiotics called magainins, first discovered in the skin of frogs, pokes holes in the walls that surround bacterial cells and thereby kills the bacteria. Other new antibiotics keep bacteria from making certain chemicals they need.

Some of the best hope for limiting future epidemics lies in integrated programs such as Roll Back Malaria, begun by the WHO in 1998. Unlike the overoptimistic program that the agency launched in 1957, Roll Back Malaria does not expect to eradicate the disease. Instead, its aim is to cut the number of malaria-related deaths in the world in half by the year 2010, then cut that second number in half by 2015. The program works to achieve this aim not only by treating malaria directly, but also by improving overall health care and health education in developing countries.

Future needs

In spite of these present or near-future improvements, infectious disease experts agree that much more needs to be done to protect the world against epidemics. One of the greatest needs is for further improvement in global networks that report disease outbreaks and related information. One badly needed surveillance system would track the spread of antibiotic-resistant microorganisms. Such a system should even track microorganisms that do not cause human disease, says Stuart Levy of Tufts University School of Medicine, because these can pass resistance genes to more dangerous microbes. Another needed surveillance system would watch for diseases that have recently spread or might spread from animals to humans. A third system might look for signs that a disease outbreak was caused by biological warfare, such as unusual genes in a disease-causing microorganism or unusual patterns or methods of disease spread.

Some experts believe that animals to be slaughtered for human consumption should not be given antibiotics or fed the remains of other animals.

More regulation, and more enforcement of existing regulations, may also be needed. Laws governing the cleanliness of domestic and imported food need to be better enforced and perhaps strengthened in the United States and other countries. Many researchers recommend that the practice of feeding animal remains to food animals be stopped. Some also feel that such animals also should not be routinely fed antibiotics. Human blood and blood products used for transfusions and medicines need to be screened dependably worldwide for HIV, hepatitis virus, and other dangerous microorganisms. Possibly, laws should limit the use of antibiotics or require health agencies to stock hypodermics that destroy themselves after a single use.

Cooperation, both between state or regional agencies and national ones and between national and international organizations, needs to increase. Wealthy nations must recognize

that, even though most infectious disease occurs in poor
countries, epidemics are a global threat from which no one
is safe. Government planners also need to cooperate with
scientists who study the effects of rising population and
environmental destruction. Programs of rural settlement
and city planning should be designed to reduce the chances
of triggering epidemics.

Perhaps the greatest need for preventing and controlling
epidemics is money. "Diversion of funds from just one B-2
bomber could have a major impact on research on new diseases," wrote Dennis Pirages, a University of Maryland

professor of government and politics, in 1996. "A significant rethinking of missions and funding is . . . long overdue."[34] Funding is needed not only for research but for training health care workers and educating the public, for vaccines and drugs, and for supplies such as one-use hypodermics. Above all, money is needed to improve health care and living conditions for the world's poor. As long as much of the world's population lives in conditions where one doctor must serve a thousand people and an injection or transfusion is as likely to give someone a deadly disease as it is to cure something, where people are packed together in miserable shacks, where streets are bathrooms and untreated sewage is dumped into drinking water, where children go hungry and are infected with a variety of microbes from birth, epidemics will flourish.

Finally, ordinary people need to take steps to protect themselves against infectious disease. In developing countries, use of tools as simple as Rita Colwell's sari-cloth filter can save thousands, perhaps millions, of lives. In developed countries, people can protect themselves and their families by doing such things as using antibiotics wisely, following safe sexual and cooking practices, and washing their hands before cooking or eating and after handling anything that might carry microbes. Such activities lack the drama of CDC workers arriving in blue space suits, but, in the long run, they may be the best way to prevent and control epidemics.

Conclusion

UNLIKE THE OPTIMISTS of the 1960s, the scientists of today recognize that infectious disease is likely to last as long as humanity—and possibly longer. "We have to come to terms with the fact that the microbial world is in competition with us,"[35] says Joshua Lederberg, who won a Nobel Prize in 1958 for his studies of bacterial genes.

Some reasons why epidemics will probably never vanish have to do with the microbes that produce them. For one thing, many disease-causing microorganisms can survive in wild animals as well as in people. Plague bacteria and hantaviruses live in or on rodents, for instance. Influenza lives in wild waterfowl, and cholera bacteria live on tiny sea creatures. Getting rid of all these animals is both impractical and undesirable, and removing their microbe passengers is likely to be equally impossible. Other bacteria and viruses, now unknown, no doubt live in still other creatures and may start causing human disease if people come into contact with them.

Even more basic is that microorganisms are constantly changing, often in unpredictable ways. Scientists once believed that disease-causing microbes would evolve to become less virulent if they remained within the human population for a long time, because the germs risked killing their offspring if they killed their human hosts. However, disease evolution expert Paul Ewald points out that a microorganism's survival is assured as long as its human host infects at least one other person before he or she dies. If the microorganism can spread quickly (as the influenza virus

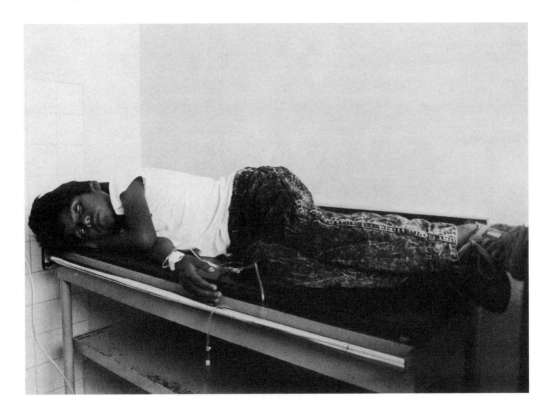

does), survive for long periods outside a host (as the anthrax bacterium can), or allow a host to remain seemingly healthy for a long period of time (as HIV does), it has little to gain by becoming mild enough to let its host live.

The nature and behavior of human beings also make an end to epidemics improbable. Unfortunately, a percentage of the human race seems likely to go on living in the conditions of poverty, crowding, malnutrition, and poor sanitation that encourage infectious disease. A percentage of personal habits and government policies seems likely to go on being shaped by greed, laziness, overconfidence, and shortsightedness. As long as these things are true, disease-causing microbes will be ready to take advantage of them.

Even if epidemics cannot be eliminated, however, they can be minimized. If governments and scientists learn to work together, if people learn to take more care of their own health and that of others around the world, the members of the "global village" will be able to react quickly

A young cholera patient in Lima, Peru, lies on a hospital stretcher while being fed intravenously.

Suspected plague carriers in New Delhi wait outside a hospital room for tests. Improved heath care and living conditions can minimize the devastation of epidemics.

when epidemics strike and, better still, keep most of them from happening at all. Infectious disease researcher George Armelagos said in 1998:

> If human beings are to overcome the current [infectious disease] crisis, it will be through sensible changes in behavior . . . combined with a commitment to stop disturbing the ecological balance of the planet. . . . We . . . bring plagues upon ourselves . . . by refusing to heed our own alarms, our own best judgment. The price of peace—or at least peaceful coexistence—with the microorganisms on this planet is eternal vigilance.[36]

Notes

Introduction

1. Quoted in Arno Karlen, *Man and Microbes: Disease and Plagues in History and Modern Times.* New York: Putnam, 1995, p. 89.

Chapter 1: Death and Victory

2. Quoted in Karlen, *Man and Microbes,* p. 117.
3. C. J. Peters and Mark Olshaker, *Virus Hunter: Thirty Years of Battling Hot Viruses Around the World.* New York: Doubleday, 1998, p. 318.
4. Quoted in Gunjan Sinha and Burkhard Bilger, "Skeletons from the Attic," *The Sciences,* September/October 1996, p. 11.
5. Quoted in Andrew Nikiforuk, *The Fourth Horseman: A Short History of Epidemics, Plagues and Other Scourges.* London: Phoenix, 1993, p. 56.
6. Quoted in Karlen, *Man and Microbes,* pp. 101–102, and Nikiforuk, *Fourth Horseman,* pp. 71–72.
7. Quoted in Elizabeth Pennisi, "U.S. Beefs Up CDC's Capabilities," *Science,* June 7, 1996, p. 1,413.

Chapter 2: Why Epidemics Are Returning

8. Nikiforuk, *Fourth Horseman,* p. xv.
9. George J. Armelagos, "The Viral Superhighway," *The Sciences,* January/February 1998, p. 24.
10. Quoted in Gary Taubes, "Apocalypse Not," *Science,* November 7, 1997, p. 1,007.
11. Armelagos, "Viral Superhighway," pp. 24+.
12. Quoted in Peter Radetsky, "Last Days of the Wonder Drugs," *Discover,* November 1998, p. 78.

13.   Quoted in Mark Caldwell, "Prokaryotes at the Gate," *Discover,* August 1994, p. 47.

Chapter 3: Emerging Epidemics

14.   Quoted in Associated Press, "AIDS Called Economic Threat in Third World," *San Francisco Chronicle,* November 28, 1997, p. A4.

15.   Quoted in Lori Oliwenstein, "Dr. Darwin," *Discover,* October 1995, pp. 112–13.

16.   Quoted in Jim Motavalli and Tracey C. Rembert, "The Trouble with Meat," *E,* May/June 1998, pp. 28+.

17.   Christopher Drew and Pam Belluck, "E. Coli Contamination Threatens Fresh Foods," *New York Times,* reprinted in *San Francisco Chronicle,* January 6, 1998.

18.   Quoted in Bruce Wallace, "Panic on the Hoof," *Maclean's,* April 8, 1996, p. 27.

19.   Quoted in Jeffrey Kluger, "Could Mad-Cow Disease Strike Here?" *Time,* January 27, 1997, p. 53.

Chapter 4: Old Killers Strike Back

20.   Quoted in Michael D. Lemonick, "Guerrilla Warfare," *Time,* Fall 1996, p. 62.

21.   Quoted in Taubes, "Apocalypse Not," p. 1,005.

22.   Quoted in Patricia Gadsby, "Fear of Flu," *Discover,* January 1999, p. 89.

23.   Quoted in Ellen Ruppel Shell, "Return of a Deadly Disease," *Atlantic,* August 1997, p. 49.

24.   Quoted in *Asiaweek,* "A Dual Scourge Hits Asia," September 29, 1995, reprinted in *World Press Review,* December 1995, p. 37.

Chapter 5: Epidemics in a Test Tube

25.   *Frontline,* "Plague War: Interview, Dr. Kanatjan Alibekov," 1998. www.pbs.org/wgbh/pages/frontline/shows/plague/interviews/alibekov.html.

26.   Leonard A. Cole, *The Eleventh Plague: The Politics of Biological and Chemical Warfare.* New York: Freeman, 1997, p. 4.

27. *Frontline,* "Plague War: Interview, Michael Osterholm," 1998. www.pbs.org/wgbh/pages/frontline/shows/plague/interviews/osterholm.html.

28. *Frontline,* "Interview: Michael Osterholm."

29. *Frontline,* "Plague War: Interview, Matthew Meselson," 1998. www.pbs.org/wgbh/pages/frontline/shows/plague/interviews/meselson.html.

Chapter 6: Tracking and Controlling Epidemics

30. Quoted in Lyric Wallwork Winik, "Before the Next Epidemic Strikes," *Parade,* February 8, 1998, p. 8.

31. Quoted in Winik, "Before the Next Epidemic Strikes," p. 7.

32. Quoted in Winik, "Before the Next Epidemic Strikes," pp. 8–9.

33. Quoted in "Global Progress," *Maclean's,* March 31, 1997, p. 56.

34. Dennis Pirages, "Microsecurity: Disease Organisms and Human Well-Being," *Current,* January 1996, p. 11.

Conclusion

35. Quoted in Judith Braffman-Miller, "Beware the Rise of Antibiotic-Resistant Microbes," *USA Today,* March 1997, p. 59.

36. Armelagos, "Viral Superhighway."

Glossary

AIDS (acquired immunodeficiency syndrome): An infectious disease, caused by the human immunodeficiency virus (HIV), that results in the collapse of the immune system.

anthrax: A bacterium-caused infectious disease that usually affects sheep and cattle but can be fatal to humans; it is a likely choice for use in biological warfare.

antibiotic: A drug that kills bacteria or stops their activity.

antibodies: Defensive mechanism produced by the immune system in response to invasion by microorganisms or other foreign substances; a different type of antibody is produced for each type of microorganism.

bacteria (plural of *bacterium*): Single-celled microorganisms, some of which can cause disease when they invade the body.

Biological Weapons Convention: A treaty prohibiting the use or stockpiling of biological weapons, first established in 1972.

BL-4: Biocontainment Level 4, the level of laboratory security required for handling microorganisms that cause fatal human diseases for which there is no treatment or vaccine.

Black Death: Bubonic plague; specifically, the plague pandemic that struck Europe in 1347.

blue suit: The space-suit-like protective clothing that workers in a BL-4 laboratory must wear.

bovine spongiform encephalopathy (BSE): A brain-destroying disease of cattle, probably caused by prions, also known as "mad cow disease."

bubonic plague: The form of the infectious disease caused by the bacterium *Yersinia pestis* that produces black, swollen lumps (buboes) on the body.

Campylobacter: A bacterium, found in uncooked chicken meat, that causes outbreaks of food poisoning.

Center for Health Applications of Aerospace Related Technologies (CHAART): An organization founded by the U.S. National Aeronautics and Space Administration (NASA) to encourage the use of satellites to track environmental factors related to infectious disease.

Centers for Disease Control and Prevention (CDC): A national agency, with headquarters in Atlanta, Georgia, that is responsible for tracking and controlling infectious disease in the United States; it also cooperates with other agencies to track and control epidemics elsewhere in the world.

cholera: An infectious disease, caused by the bacterium *Vibrio cholerae,* that causes vomiting and diarrhea so severe that a victim can die from loss of body water within a day or so.

conjugation: A sexlike process by which bacteria can exchange genes.

contagious disease: A disease that can be spread from one living thing to another by direct or indirect contact.

cowpox (vaccinia): A mild disease produced by a virus closely related to the one that causes smallpox; a person who has had cowpox is immune to smallpox.

Creutzfeldt-Jakob disease (CJD): A fatal human brain disease probably caused by prions; one form of it is possibly spread by eating beef from cattle suffering from bovine spongiform encephalopathy.

crowd disease: An infectious disease that spreads easily in crowds and requires crowds to maintain itself.

Cyclospora: A microorganism that can infect uncooked fruit and cause food poisoning.

DDT: Dichloro-diphenyl-trichloroethane, a powerful insecticide discovered in the 1940s.

deer mouse: A rodent, common in the United States, that often carries the Sin Nombre hantavirus.

Directly Observed Treatment, Short Course (DOTS): A tuberculosis treatment procedure in which a health care worker or family member observes a sick person to make sure that he or she takes prescribed antibiotics during each day of a six-month treatment period.

Ebola fever: An infectious viral disease that causes severe bleeding from every organ and body opening and kills up to 90 percent of its victims within a few days.

emerging disease: An infectious disease that has recently gained the power to infect human beings or has recently greatly extended the area in which it occurs or the number of cases of illness it causes.

Enterococcus faecalis: A bacterium, common in hospitals, that can cause moderately serious infections; some strains of it have a gene for resistance to the "last resort" antibiotic vancomycin.

epi-aid (epidemic aid): An assignment in which a team from the CDC or a similar agency is sent to help local health workers track and control an epidemic.

epidemic: An event in which the number of cases of an infectious disease in a certain area rises rapidly until almost everyone in the area has been infected.

epidemiology: The branch of medicine that studies how diseases spread and why certain diseases affect some people but not others.

eradicate: To wipe out completely.

Escherichia coli (E. coli): A bacterium that usually lives harmlessly in the human intestine; one new strain of it can cause severe food poisoning.

evolution: The process by which generations of living things change in response to changes in their environment.

flesh-eating strep: Common name for necrotizing fasciitis, a rare, severe infection caused by streptococcus A bacteria.

gene: A unit of inherited information contained in a cell.

genome: The complete collection of genes found in each cell of a living thing.

germ: Microorganism, especially one that can cause disease in humans.

germ theory of disease: The idea, first proposed in the late nineteenth century, that particular infectious diseases are caused by particular types of microorganisms.

hantavirus: One of a family of viruses that lives in rodents and sometimes causes severe illness in humans.

hepatitis: Any one of several diseases, caused by different viruses, that damage the liver.

HIV (human immunodeficiency virus): The virus that causes AIDS.

hypodermic syringe: A device, consisting of a plunger, a hollow tube, and a needle, used for injecting fluids into the body.

immune: Resistant to an infectious disease because of previous exposure to (the microorganism that causes) it, either by having had the disease or by having received its microorganism in a vaccine.

immune system: The defense system by which the body naturally resists infectious disease.

immunity: Resistance to an infectious disease, produced by the immune system after it is exposed to the type of microorganism that causes the disease.

infect: Invade the body, regardless of whether the invasion causes sickness.

infectious disease: A disease caused by a small living entity, usually a microorganism, that invades the body of a larger living being.

influenza: An infectious disease, caused by a virus, that chiefly affects the respiratory (breathing) system; most forms are mild, but some are deadly.

influenza A (H5N1): A new strain of influenza virus that caused an outbreak of severe disease in chickens and a few humans in Hong Kong in 1997.

insecticide: A chemical that kills insects.

Lyme disease: An infectious disease that is caused by a bacterium and spread by ticks that live on deer; if untreated, the disease can result in severe joint and heart damage.

mad cow disease: Popular name for bovine spongiform encephalitis.

magainin: One of a new family of antibiotics that pokes holes in bacterial cell walls, killing the bacteria.

malaria: An infectious disease, caused by a microorganism, that destroys red blood cells and is spread by the bite of mosquitoes.

megacity: A city with a population of more than ten million.

microbe: A microorganism, especially one that causes disease in humans.

microorganism: A living thing too small to see without a microscope.

mutation: A change in a gene, produced by chance or by environmental factors.

National Center for Infectious Diseases (NCID): The agency within the CDC that deals with epidemics.

necrotizing fasciitis: A rare disease, caused by streptococcus A bacteria, in which flesh is rapidly destroyed; popularly called flesh-eating strep.

outbreak: A small epidemic or cluster of cases of an infectious disease.

pandemic: An epidemic that affects the whole world, or large parts of it, at about the same time.

plague: Sometimes, any epidemic disease; specifically, the infectious disease caused by the bacterium *Yersinia pestis* (bubonic or pneumonic plague).

pneumonic plague: A form of the *Yersinia pestis*–caused infectious disease that affects the lungs and can be spread through the air.

prion: An abnormal form of a brain protein that can cause infectious diseases that destroy the brain.

ProMED (Program to Monitor Emerging Diseases): A surveillance network that allows health professionals to share information about outbreaks of emerging disease by means of the Internet.

quarantine: A procedure by which people who are or might be suffering from an infectious disease are isolated to keep them from spreading the disease.

Salmonella: A genus of bacteria that can cause severe food poisoning.

Seoul virus: A hantavirus that infects rats in slums and can cause severe bleeding in the kidneys of humans.

Sin Nombre virus: A recently discovered hantavirus that caused an outbreak of lung-destroying illness in the American Southwest in 1993.

smallpox: An infectious disease, caused by a virus, that is often fatal and can leave survivors blind or severely scarred.

spore: A form of certain bacteria, such as the ones that cause anthrax, that can survive for long periods outside a living body and is very difficult to destroy.

Staphylococcus aureus: A type of bacterium, common in hospitals, that can cause severe infections of wounds and surgical incisions; called staph for short.

strain: A subtype of a particular kind of microorganism.

streptococcus: A common bacterium that can cause a variety of human diseases, including infections of wounds and surgical incisions; called strep for short.

sulfa drugs: Drugs made from a chemical called sulfanilamide, invented in the 1930s, that kill several types of bacteria.

symptom: A sign of illness, such as coughing or vomiting.

syphilis: A serious sexually transmitted infectious disease, caused by a bacterium.

tuberculosis: A serious infectious disease, caused by a bacterium, that primarily affects the lungs of people weakened by malnutrition or other illnesses.

United States Army Medical Research Institute of Infectious Diseases (USAMRIID): A military agency responsible for the protection of American soldiers against infectious diseases.

vaccination: A process by which weakened or killed microorganisms of a type that causes an infectious disease are put into the body in order to make the immune system produce resistance to that disease.

vancomycin: An antibiotic that can kill most, but not all, bacteria that are resistant to other antibiotics.

Vibrio cholerae: The bacterium that causes cholera.

virulent: Capable of causing serious illness and death.

virus: A microscopic agent, on the borderline between living and nonliving things, consisting of genes inside a protein shell; some viruses cause infectious diseases in humans.

World Health Organization (WHO): An international organization that works to improve the health of the world; its activities include preventing, tracking, and controlling epidemics.

yellow fever: A serious infectious disease that is caused by a virus and spread by the bite of mosquitoes; sometimes called yellow jack.

Yersinia pestis: The bacterium that causes bubonic and pneumonic plague.

Organizations
to Contact

American Lung Association
1740 Broadway, Suite 202
New York, NY 10019-4315
(212) 315-8700 or (800) 586-4872
e-mail: info@lungusa.org
Internet: www.lungusa.org

This large organization supports research on lung diseases, including influenza and tuberculosis, and educates health professionals and patients about these diseases. It offers brochures, pamphlets, and videos.

American Society of Tropical Medicine and Hygiene
60 Revere Drive, Suite 500
Northbrook, IL 60061
(847) 480-9592
e-mail: astmh@astmh.org
Internet: www.astmh.org

This professional organization studies tropical diseases, including those that are infectious, viral, or insect borne. Its publications include a brochure, "Health Hints for the Tropics," and a bimonthly newsletter. Its website offers links to other sites with information on tropical diseases as well as teaching modules on tropical disease.

Body Positive
19 Fulton Street, Suite 308B
New York, NY 10038
(800) 566-6599

Provides support services for people with HIV/AIDS and their families and friends. Publishes a monthly newsletter, *Body Positive.*

CDC National Prevention Information Network

Box 6003
Rockville, MD 20849-6003
(800) 458-5231
e-mail: ailsinfo@cdcnac.org
Internet: www.cdcnpin.org

Provides information on AIDS. Offers brochures on such topics as AIDS and minorities and AIDS and tuberculosis.

National Association of People with AIDS

1413 K Street NW, Seventh Floor
Washington, DC 20005-3442
(202) 898-0414
e-mail: napwa@napwa.org
Internet: www.napwa.org

Provides information on health care and advocacy issues related to AIDS and education programs for people infected with or at risk for infection with HIV and their loved ones. Brochures include "An Ounce of Prevention," "Facts About AIDS," and "Living with HIV."

National Center for Infectious Diseases

Centers for Disease Control and Prevention
1600 Clifton Road NE
Atlanta, GA 30333
(770) 488-1815 (CDC general number)
Internet: www.cdc.gov/ncidod/index.htm

This organization, part of the Centers for Disease Control and Prevention, works to track and control infectious disease. It offers a wide variety of brochures, including ones on cholera, Ebola fever, and hantavirus infection.

National Institute of Allergy and Infectious Diseases

Office of Communications and Public Liaison
Building 31, Room 7A-50
31 Center Drive MSC 2520
Bethesda, MD 20892-2520

(301) 496-4000 (NIH general number)
Internet: www.niaid.nih.gov

NIAID, part of the National Institutes of Health, researches allergies and infectious diseases. It offers publications on subjects including AIDS, emerging infectious diseases, malaria, tuberculosis, influenza, and food-borne illnesses.

Society of Healthcare Epidemiologists of America
19 Mantua Road
Mount Royal, NJ 08061
(609) 423-0087
e-mail: sheahg@shea.smarthub.com

Works to improve treatment results in hospitals and other healthcare settings, including prevention and control of hospital infections. Publishes a monthly journal, *Infection Control and Hospital Epidemiology.*

Teens Teaching AIDS Prevention
3030 Walnut
Kansas City, MO 64108
(800) 234-8336
e-mail: teenstap@concentric.net

Provides teenagers with information on AIDS prevention through peer counseling. Offers brochures and manuals.

World Health Organization (WHO)
Avenue Appia
CH-1211
Geneva 27, Switzerland
011-41-22-791-2111
e-mail: info@who.ch
Internet: www.who.int/home/map_ht.html

Founded in 1948 and a part of the United Nations, WHO works for world health, including control of infectious diseases. Its website offers information on the organization and its programs.

Suggestions for Further Reading

Books

Leonard A. Cole, *The Eleventh Plague: The Politics of Biological and Chemical Warfare.* New York: Freeman, 1997. Describes modern history of chemical and biological weapons, including American tests using "harmless" bacteria, and expresses hope that global disgust with such weapons will keep them from being used.

Phyllis Corzine, *The Black Death.* San Diego, CA: Lucent Books, 1997. Discusses the profound social, psychological, political, spiritual, and economic changes in medieval Europe brought about by the plague.

Jacqueline L. Harris, *Communicable Diseases.* New York: TFC Books, 1993. Book for young people describing contagious diseases caused by different types of microbes, including how they are spread and how they are treated.

Arno Karlen, *Man and Microbes: Disease and Plagues in History and Modern Times.* New York: Putnam, 1995. Focuses on history of past epidemics but also describes the present threat of emerging and the returning epidemic diseases.

C. J. Peters and Mark Olshaker, *Virus Hunter: Thirty Years of Battling Hot Viruses Around the World.* New York: Doubleday, 1998. Exciting account of Peters's career at USAMRIID, the military equivalent of the CDC, during which he tracked Ebola and other dangerous viruses in many parts of the world.

Richard Preston, *The Hot Zone.* New York: Doubleday, 1995. Best-selling description of the outbreak of Ebola fever among monkeys in Reston, Virginia, in late 1989, and the fear that it would start a human epidemic.

Lori Shein, *AIDS*. San Diego, CA: Lucent Books, 1998. Traces discovery of the epidemic and discusses the challenges, triumphs, and failures of prevention and treatment efforts.

Periodicals

Shannon Brownlee, "The Disease Busters," *U.S. News & World Report,* March 27, 1995.

Jared Diamond, "The Arrow of Disease," *Discover,* October 1992.

Laurie Garrett, "The Return of Infectious Disease," *Foreign Affairs,* January/February 1996.

Peter Jaret, "Viruses," *National Geographic,* July 1994.

Mark Witten, "Outbreak on 14-North," *Saturday Night,* May 1996.

Websites

Anatomy of an Epidemic (library.advanced.org/11170). Shows an animated map of the world; viewer can select a disease and watch it spread across its range.

Medscape (www.medscape.com/Home/Topics/ID/ InfectiousDiseases.htm/). Includes patient resources on topics such as tuberculosis and viral hepatitis as well as links to other sites related to infectious disease, including several from CDC and WHO.

Outbreak (www.outbreak.org). Provides information on emerging diseases.

Pfizer Microbes Site (www.Pfizer.com/rd/microbes). Provides an interesting description of exhibits in the drug company's touring museum show about disease-causing microorganisms and their effects on history.

ProMED (Program for Monitoring Infectious Diseases) (www.fas.org/promed). This program, sponsored by the Federation of American Scientists, monitors infectious diseases worldwide. Its website includes links to other infectious disease sites, mapped resources for combating infectious disease, and recommended reading.

Works Consulted

Books

Laurie Garrett, *The Coming Plague: Newly Emerging Diseases in a World Out of Balance.* New York: Penguin, 1995. Long but fascinating account of emerging and returning epidemic diseases and the people who travel around the world to investigate them.

Joseph B. McCormick and Susan Fisher-Hoch, *Level 4: Virus Hunters of the CDC.* Atlanta: Turner Publishing, 1996. McCormick, former chief of the CDC's Special Pathogens Branch, and Fisher-Hoch, his wife and fellow infectious disease investigator, describe their experiences in stalking the world's most deadly viruses, including the Ebola fever virus and HIV.

Andrew Nikiforuk, *The Fourth Horseman: A Short History of Epidemics, Plagues and Other Scourges.* London: Phoenix, 1993. Describes the past history and present activity of epidemic diseases such as plague, malaria, smallpox, influenza, and tuberculosis.

Christopher Wills, *Yellow Fever, Black Goddess.* Reading, MA: Addison-Wesley/Helix, 1996. Tells how interactions between humans and disease-causing microbes have shaped the evolution of both.

Charles-Edward Amory Winslow, *The Conquest of Epidemic Disease: A Chapter in the History of Ideas.* Madison: University of Wisconsin Press, 1980. Provides many quotes from primary sources to show how thinking about the cause of infectious diseases changed from ancient times to the end of the nineteenth century.

Periodicals

George J. Armelagos, "The Viral Superhighway," *The Sciences,* January/February 1998.

Associated Press, "AIDS Called Economic Threat in Third World," *San Francisco Chronicle,* November 28, 1997.

————, "FDA Approves First Vaccine to Combat Lyme Disease," *San Francisco Chronicle,* December 22, 1998.

————, "The Problem with Today's Food System," *San Francisco Chronicle,* December 10, 1997.

————, "Supergerm Suspected in N.Y. Man's Death," *San Francisco Chronicle,* April 25, 1998.

Judith Braffman-Miller, "Beware the Rise of Antibiotic-Resistant Microbes," *USA Today,* March 1997.

Eric Brazil, "Monitoring of Imported Food Deemed Ineffective," *San Francisco Examiner/Chronicle,* May 10, 1998.

Susan Brink, with Dana Coleman, "Global Epidemics, Close to Home," *U.S. News & World Report,* October 28, 1996.

Shannon Brownlee and others, "Horror in the Hot Zone," *U.S. News & World Report,* May 22, 1995.

Geoff Butcher, " 'Million Murdering Death': How Malaria Has Impacted Mankind's Progress," *History Today,* April 1998.

Mark Caldwell, "Ebola Tamed—For Now," *Discover,* January 1996.

————, "Prokaryotes at the Gate," *Discover,* August 1994.

————, "Vigil for a Doomed Virus," *Discover,* March 1992.

Marjorie Centofanti, "Playing by the Rules: How and Why Organisms Turn Nasty," *Science News,* December 2, 1995.

Rita R. Colwell, "Global Climate and Infectious Disease: The Cholera Paradigm," *Science,* December 20, 1996.

Cox News Service, "Rising Number of Patients Get Sicker at Hospital," *San Francisco Chronicle,* March 12, 1998.

"Deliberate Resistance," *Discover,* April 1996.

Andrew P. Dobson and E. Robin Carper, "Infectious Diseases and Human Population History," *BioScience,* February 1996.

Catherine Dold, "The Cholera Lesson," *Discover,* February 1999.

Christopher Drew and Pam Belluck, "E. Coli Contamination Threatens Fresh Foods," *New York Times,* reprinted in *San Francisco Chronicle,* January 6, 1998.

"A Dual Scourge Hits Asia," *Asiaweek* (Hong Kong), September 29, 1995, reprinted in *World Press Review,* December 1995.

Paul W. Ewald, "On Darwin, Snow, and Deadly Diseases," *Natural History,* June 1994.

Tom Fennell, "Stalking a Killer Virus," *Maclean's,* January 12, 1998.

Dan Ferber, "New Hunt for the Roots of Resistance," *Science,* April 3, 1998.

Patricia Gadsby, "Fear of Flu," *Discover,* January 1999.

Geoffrey P. Garnett and Edward C. Holmes, "The Ecology of Emergent Infectious Disease," *BioScience,* February 1996.

Nancy Gibbs, "In Search of the Dying," *Time,* May 29, 1995.

R. I. Glass, M. Libel, and A. D. Brandling-Bennett, "Epidemic Cholera in the Americas," *Science,* June 12, 1992.

Josie Glausiusz, "Case Closed," *Discover,* January 1998.

———, "The Frog Solution," *Discover,* November 1998.

"Global Progress," *Maclean's,* March 31, 1997.

Stephen Jay Gould, "Above All, Do No Harm," *Natural History,* October 1998.

Denise Grady, "Death at the Corners," *Discover,* December 1993.

Horst Güntheroth, "Ebola: Death in the Jungle," *Stern* (Germany), May 18, 1995, reprinted in *World Press Review,* August 1995.

Carl T. Hall, "Health Study Reports 10% Increase in AIDS Infections Worldwide," *San Francisco Chronicle,* November 24, 1998.

Christy Hanson, "Imagine Victory over Tuberculosis," *World Health,* March/April 1995.

David L. Heymann, "Controlling Epidemic Diseases," *World Health,* November/December 1996.

Reynolds Holding and William Carlsen, "Deadly Needles," *San Francisco Chronicle,* October 27–29, 1998.

Nicholas Horrock, "The New Terror Fear: Biological Weapons," *U.S. News & World Report,* May 12, 1997.

Leslie Alan Horvitz, "It's a War to Restore Antibiotics," *Insight,* March 18, 1996.

Beatrice Trum Hunter, "Multidrug Resistance to a Virulent Pathogen," *Consumers' Research,* July 1998.

———, "Overlooked Threats of Foodborne Illness," *Consumers' Research,* October 1995.

Carol Kahn, "Our Fight to Stop Those Deadly Bugs," *Parade,* December 20, 1998.

Jeffrey Kluger, "Could Mad-Cow Disease Strike Here?" *Time,* January 27, 1997.

Robert Koenig, "Koch Keeps New Watch on Infections," *Science,* June 7, 1996.

———, "A Shared European Concern," *Science,* June 7, 1996.

Erik Larson, "The Flu Hunters," *Time,* February 23, 1998.

Michael D. Lemonick, "Guerrilla Warfare," *Time,* Fall 1996.

Eugene Linden, "Global Fever," *Time,* July 8, 1996.

Charles L. Mee Jr., "How a Mysterious Disease Laid Low Europe's Masses," *Smithsonian,* February 1990.

Francois-Xavier Meslin, Klaus Stohr, and P. Formenty, "Emerging Zoonoses," *World Health,* January/February 1997.

Jim Motavalli and Tracey C. Rembert, "The Trouble with Meat," *E,* May/June 1998.

Kieran Mulvaney, "Mad Cows and the Colonies: It Can't Happen Here?" *E,* July/August 1996.

David N. Nabarro and Elizabeth M. Taylor, "The 'Roll Back Malaria' Campaign," *Science,* June 26, 1998.

Lauran Neergaard, "Polio Eradication Possible by 2000," *San Francisco Examiner/Chronicle,* May 3, 1998.

Lori Oliwenstein, "Dr. Darwin," *Discover,* October 1995.

Wendy Orent, "Escape from Moscow," *The Sciences,* May/June 1998.

Elizabeth Pennisi, "U.S. Beefs Up CDC's Capabilities," *Science,* June 7, 1998.

David Pimentel and others, "Ecology of Increasing Disease: Population Growth and Environmental Degradation," *BioScience,* October 1998.

Dennis Pirages, "Microsecurity: Disease Organisms and Human Well-Being," *Current,* January 1996.

Morris E. Potter, Yasmin Motarjemi, and Fritz K. Kaferstein, "Emerging Foodborne Diseases," *World Health,* January/February 1997.

Stanley B. Prusiner, "Prion Diseases and the BSE Crisis," *Science,* October 10, 1997.

Peter Radetsky, "Last Days of the Wonder Drugs," *Discover,* November 1998.

Janet Raloff, "How Climate Perturbations Can Plague Us," *Science News,* September 23, 1995.

Sarah Richardson, "The Return of the Plague," *Discover,* January 1995.

————, "Tabloid Strep," *Discover,* January 1995.

Guenael Rodier, "WHO Response to Epidemics," *World Health,* January/February 1997.

Patrick Rogers and John Wright, "This Terrible Madness," *People,* April 22, 1996.

Philip E. Ross, "A New Black Death?" *Forbes,* September 12, 1994.

Sabin Russell, "Disease Has 50% Death Rate, and No Drug Can Fight It," *San Francisco Chronicle,* July 4, 1995.

Vincent J. Schodolski and V. Dion Haynes, "Mail-Order Bubonic Plague Leads to Stricter Rules," *Chicago Tribune,* reprinted in *San Francisco Examiner/Chronicle,* March 1, 1998.

N. Seppa, "Ebola Virus Vaccine Protects Guinea Pigs," *Science News,* January 10, 1998.

Robert F. Service, "Antibiotics That Resist Resistance," *Science,* November 3, 1995.

Ellen Ruppel Shell, "Resurgence of a Deadly Disease," *Atlantic,* August 1997.

Gunjan Sinha and Burkhard Bilger, "Skeletons from the Attic," *The Sciences,* September/October 1996.

S. Sternberg, "Human Version of Mad Cow Disease?" *Science News,* April 13, 1996.

Gary Taubes, "Apocalypse Not," *Science,* November 7, 1997.

———, "Malarial Dreams," *Discover,* March 1998.

Michael Taylor, "$1.5 Million Federal Fine for Odwalla," *San Francisco Chronicle,* July 24, 1998.

J. Travis, "Genome Sequence Aids War on Tuberculosis," *Science News,* June 13, 1998.

———, "Spying Diseases from the Sky," *Science News,* August 2, 1997.

Bruce Wallace, "Panic on the Hoof," *Maclean's,* April 8, 1996.

Ellen Wallace, "Africa's Deadly Visitor," *People,* May 29, 1995.

Barbara Wickens, "History's Scourge," *Maclean's,* October 10, 1994.

Samuel L. Wilson, "Pandora's Bite," *Natural History,* July 1991.

Lyric Wallwork Winik, "Before the Next Epidemic Strikes," *Parade,* February 8, 1998.

Tim Zimmerman, "Fighting TB: A Second Chance to Do It Right," *U.S. News & World Report,* March 31, 1997.

Internet Sources

Frontline, "Plague War" (several interviews and other articles). 1998. www.pbs.org/wgbh/pages/frontline/shows/plague.html.

Index

oral rehydration therapy, 50
overcrowding, 26

Parker, Janet, 60
Pasteur, Louis, 19, 20, 21
penicillin, 23, 80
Peters, C. J., 10, 61
plague. *See* Black Death; bubonic plague
Plague of Athens, 11–12
polio
    eradication effort, 75–76
poverty, 25–26, 83
prions, 45, 47
ProMED (Program to Monitor Emerging
    Diseases), 79

quarantine, 14

rabies vaccine, 21
refugees, 26
Robert Koch Institute, 74
Roll Back Malaria, 80

Salmonella, 43
Seoul virus, 41
simian hemorrhagic fever, 61
Sin Nombre virus, 40–41
Slaughterhouse (Eisnitz), 43
smallpox
    development of vaccination for, 20–21
    introduction into Americas, 15–17, 64
    last recorded death from, 60
Snow, John, 19, 21, 50
Soviet Union
    biological weapons research by, 63, 65–66
"Spanish flu," 22
Staphylococcus aureus, 52
streptococcus type A, 52
Sudan
    Ebola outbreak in, 37
sulfanilamide (sulfa) drugs, 23
surveillance
    for new influenza strains, 54, 76

tetanus, 75
Time magazine, 47
travel
    and Indian plague, 11
    as means of spreading microbes, 11, 12,
        27–28

tuberculosis (TB), 10, 75
    DOTS treatment system for, 79
    identification of cause of, 20
    method of spread of, 57
    resurgence of, 58, 59

United Nations, 26
    AIDS program, 37, 76
    Intergovernmental Panel on Climate
        Change, 28
U.S. Army Medical Research Institute of
    Infectious Diseases, 61, 62, 73

vaccines/vaccination, 22
    first development of, 20
    microbe resistance to, 32–33
    research in, 76–77
vaccinia (cowpox), 20
vancomycin, 80
    microbe resistance to, 53
Vibrio cholerae, 18
viruses
    development of resistance by, 32

weather
    role in epidemics, 28
        Sin Nombre virus, 41
    satellite tracking of, 78
WHO. *See* World Health Organization
whooping cough, 75
World Health Organization (WHO), 23,
    30–31
    on disease spread by needles, 29
    on drug-resistant tuberculosis, 59
    in Ebola fever outbreak, 38
    malaria eradication campaign, 56, 80
    on tuberculosis infections/deaths
        worldwide, 57–58
    vaccination programs, 75
Worldwatch Institute, 26
World Wide Web, 79

yellow fever, 17–18, 22
Yeltsin, Boris, 63
Yersinia pestis, 12, 33

Zaire
    Ebola outbreak in, 37–38

Picture Credits

About the Author

Lisa Yount earned a bachelor's degree with honors in English and creative writing from Stanford University. She has a lifelong interest in biology and medicine. She has been a professional writer for more than thirty years, producing educational materials, magazine articles, and more than twenty books for young people. Her books for Lucent include *Memory, Biomedical Ethics,* and *Cancer.* She lives in El Cerrito, California, with her husband, a large library, and several cats.